BMC COMPETITIONS DEPARTMENT
SECRETS

AF000657

Also from Veloce Publishing

Those Were The Days ... Series
Alpine Trials & Rallies 1910-1973 (Pfundner)
American 'Independent' Automakers – AMC to Willys 1945 to 1960 (Mort)
Anglo-American Cars from the 1930s to the 1970s (Mort)
Austins, The last real (Peck)
Brighton National Speed Trials (Gardiner)
British Touring Car Racing (Collins)
British Police Cars (Walker)
British Woodies (Peck)
Don Hayter's MGB Story – The birth of the MGB in MG's Abingdon Design & Development Office (Hayter)
Endurance Racing at Silverstone in the 1970s & 1980s (Parker)
Hot Rod & Stock Car Racing in Britain in the 1980s (Neil)
Last Real Austins 1946-1959, The (Peck)
MG's Abingdon Factory (Moylan)
Motor Racing at Brands Hatch in the Seventies (Parker)
Motor Racing at Brands Hatch in the Eighties (Parker)
Motor Racing at Crystal Palace (Collins)
Motor Racing at Goodwood in the Sixties (Gardiner)
Motor Racing at Nassau in the 1950s & 1960s (O'Neil)
Motor Racing at Oulton Park in the 1960s (McFadyen)
Motor Racing at Oulton Park in the 1970s (McFadyen)
Motor Racing at Thruxton in the 1970s (Grant-Braham)
Motor Racing at Thruxton in the 1980s (Grant-Braham)
Superprix – The Story of Birmingham Motor Race (Page & Collins)
Three Wheelers (Bobbitt)

Great Cars
Austin-Healey – A celebration of the fabulous 'Big' Healey (Piggott)
Triumph TR - TR2 to 6: The last of the traditional sports cars (Piggott)

Rally Giants Series
Audi Quattro (Robson)
Austin Healey 100-6 & 3000 (Robson)
Fiat 131 Abarth (Robson)
Ford Escort MkI (Robson)
Ford Escort RS Cosworth & World Rally Car (Robson)
Ford Escort RS1800 (Robson)
Lancia Delta 4WD/Integrale (Robson)
Lancia Stratos (Robson)
Mini Cooper/Mini Cooper S (Robson)
Peugeot 205 T16 (Robson)
Saab 96 & V4 (Robson)
Subaru Impreza (Robson)
Toyota Celica GT4 (Robson)

WSC Giants
Audi R8 (Wagstaff)
Ferrari 312P & 312PB (Collins & McDonough)
Gulf-Mirage 1967 to 1982 (McDonough)
Matra Sports Cars – MS620, 630, 650, 660 & 670 – 1966 to 1974 (McDonough)

Biographies
A Chequered Life – Graham Warner and the Chequered Flag (Hesletine)
A Life Awheel – The 'auto' biography of W de Forte (Skelton)
Amédée Gordini ... a true racing legend (Smith)
André Lefebvre, and the cars he created at Voisin and Citroën (Beck)
Chris Carter at Large – Stories from a lifetime in motorcycle racing (Carter & Skelton)
Cliff Allison, The Official Biography of – From the Fells to Ferrari (Gauld)
Edward Turner – The Man Behind the Motorcycles (Clew)
Driven by Desire – The Desiré Wilson Story
First Principles – The Official Biography of Keith Duckworth (Burr)
Inspired to Design – F1 cars, Indycars & racing tyres: the autobiography of Nigel Bennett (Bennett)
Jack Sears, The Official Biography of – Gentleman Jack (Gauld)
Jim Redman – 6 Times World Motorcycle Champion: The Autobiography (Redman)
John Chatham – 'Mr Big Healey' – The Official Biography (Burr)
The Lee Noble Story (Wilkins)
Mason's Motoring Mayhem – Tony Mason's hectic life in motorsport and television (Mason)
Raymond Mays' Magnificent Obsession (Apps)
Pat Moss Carlsson Story, The – Harnessing Horsepower (Turner)
'Sox' – Gary Hocking – the forgotten World Motorcycle Champion (Hughes)
Tony Robinson – The biography of a race mechanic (Wagstaff)
Virgil Exner – Visioneer: The Official Biography of Virgil M Exner Designer Extraordinaire (Grist)

General
1½-litre GP Racing 1961-1965 (Whitelock)
AC Two-litre Saloons & Buckland Sportscars (Archibald)
Alfa Romeo 155/156/147 Competition Touring Cars (Collins)
Alfa Romeo Giulia Coupé GT & GTA (Tipler)
Alfa Romeo Montreal – The dream car that came true (Taylor)
Alfa Romeo Montreal – The Essential Companion (Classic Reprint of 500 copies) (Taylor)
Alfa Tipo 33 (McDonough & Collins)
Alpine & Renault – The Development of the Revolutionary Turbo F1 Car 1968 to 1979 (Smith)
Alpine & Renault – The Sports Prototypes 1963 to 1969 (Smith)
Alpine & Renault – The Sports Prototypes 1973 to 1978 (Smith)
Anatomy of the Classic Mini (Huthert & Ely)
Anatomy of the Works Minis (Moylan)
Armstrong-Siddeley (Smith)
Art Deco and British Car Design (Down)
Automotive A-Z, Lane's Dictionary of Automotive Terms (Lane)
Automotive Mascots (Kay & Springate)
Bahamas Speed Weeks, The (O'Neil)
Bentley Continental, Corniche and Azure (Bennett)
Bentley MkVI, Rolls-Royce Silver Wraith, Dawn & Cloud/Bentley R & S-Series (Nutland)
Bluebird CN7 (Stevens)
BMW 5-Series (Cranswick)
BMW Z-Cars (Taylor)
British at Indianapolis, The (Wagstaff)
British Cars, The Complete Catalogue of, 1895-1975 (Culshaw & Horrobin)
BRM – A Mechanic's Tale (Salmon)
BRM V16 (Ludvigsen)
Bugatti Type 40 (Price)
Bugatti 46/50 Updated Edition (Price & Arbey)
Bugatti T44 & T49 (Price & Arbey)
Bugatti 57 2nd Edition (Price)
Bugatti Type 57 Grand Prix – A Celebration (Tomlinson)
Carrera Panamericana, La (Tipler)
Car-tastrophes – 80 automotive atrocities from the past 20 years (Honest John, Fowler)
Chrysler 300 – America's Most Powerful Car 2nd Edition (Ackerson)
Chrysler PT Cruiser (Ackerson)
Citroën DS (Bobbitt)
Classic British Car Electrical Systems (Astley)
Cobra – The Real Thing! (Legate)
Competition Car Aerodynamics 3rd Edition (McBeath)
Competition Car Composites A Practical Handbook (Revised 2nd Edition) (McBeath)
Concept Cars, How to illustrate and design (Dewey)
Cortina – Ford's Bestseller (Robson)
Cosworth - The Search for Power (6th edition) (Robson)
Coventry Climax Racing Engines (Hammill)
Daily Mirror 1970 World Cup Rally 40, The (Robson)
Daimler SP250 New Edition (Long)
Datsun Fairlady Roadster to 280ZX – The Z-Car Story (Long)
Dino – The V6 Ferrari (Long)
Dodge Challenger & Plymouth Barracuda (Grist)
Dodge Charger – Enduring Thunder (Ackerson)
Dodge Dynamite! (Grist)
Dorset from the Sea – The Jurassic Coast from Lyme Regis to Old Harry Rocks photographed from its best viewpoint (also Souvenir Edition) (Belasco)
Draw & Paint Cars – How to (Gardiner)
Drive on the Wild Side, A – 20 Extreme Driving Adventures From Around the World (Weaver)
Fast Ladies – Female Racing Drivers 1888 to 1970 (Bouzanquet)
Fate of the Sleeping Beauties, The (op de Weegh/Hottendorff/op de Weegh)
Ferrari 288 GTO, The Book of the (Sackey)
Ferrari 333 SP (O'Neil)
Fiat & Abarth 124 Spider & Coupé (Tipler)
Fiat & Abarth 500 & 600 – 2nd Edition (Bobbitt)
Fiats, Great Small (Ward)
Ford Cleveland 335-Series V8 engine 1970 to 1982 – The Essential Source Book (Hammill)
Ford F100/F150 Pick-up 1948-1996 (Ackerson)
Ford F150 Pick-up 1997-2005 (Ackerson)
Ford GT – Then, and Now (Streather)
Ford GT40 (Legate)
Ford Midsize Muscle – Fairlane, Torino & Ranchero (Cranswick)
Ford Model Y (Roberts)
Ford Small Block V8 Racing Engines 1962-1970 – The Essential Source Book (Hammill)
Ford Thunderbird From 1954, The Book of the (Long)
Formula 5000 Motor Racing, Back then ... and back now (Lawson)
Forza Minardi! (Vigar)
France: the essential guide for car enthusiasts – 200 things for the car enthusiast to see and do (Parish)
Grand Prix Ferrari – The Years of Enzo Ferrari's Power, 1948-1980 (Pritchard)
Grand Prix Ford – DFV-powered Formula 1 Cars (Robson)
GT – The World's Best GT Cars 1953-73 (Dawson)
Hillclimbing & Sprinting – The Essential Manual (Short & Wilkinson)
Honda NSX (Long)
Inside the Rolls-Royce & Bentley Styling Department – 1971 to 2001 (Hull)
Intermeccanica – The Story of the Prancing Bull (McCredie & Reisner)
Jaguar, The Rise of (Price)
Jaguar XJ 220 – The Inside Story (Moreton)
Jaguar XJ-S, The Book of the (Long)
Jeep CJ (Ackerson)
Jeep Wrangler (Ackerson)
The Jowett Jupiter - The car that leaped to fame (Nankivell)
Karmann-Ghia Coupé & Convertible (Bobbitt)
Kris Meeke – Intercontinental Rally Challenge Champion (McBride)
Lamborghini Miura Bible, The (Sackey)
Lamborghini Urraco, The Book of the (Landsem)
Lambretta Bible, The (Davies)
Lancia 037 (Collins)
Lancia Delta HF Integrale (Blaettel & Wagner)
Land Rover Series III Reborn (Porter)
Land Rover, The Half-ton Military (Cook)
Le Mans Panoramic (Ireland)
Lexus Story, The (Long)
Lola – The Illustrated History (1957-1977) (Starkey)
Lola – All the Sports Racing & Single-seater Racing Cars 1978-1997 (Starkey)
Lola T70 – The Racing History & Individual Chassis Record – 4th Edition (Starkey)
Lotus 18 Colin Chapman's U-turn (Whitelock)
Lotus 49 (Oliver)
Maserati 250F In Focus (Pritchard)
Mazda MX-5/Miata 1.6 Enthusiast's Workshop Manual (Grainger & Shoemark)
Mazda MX-5/Miata 1.8 Enthusiast's Workshop Manual (Grainger & Shoemark)
Mazda MX-5 Miata, The book of the – The 'Mk1' NA-series 1988 to 1997 (Long)
Mazda MX-5 Miata Roadster (Long)
Mazda Rotary-engined Cars (Cranswick)
Maximum Mini (Booij)
Mercedes-Benz SL – R230 series 2001 to 2011 (Long)
Mercedes-Benz SL – W113-series 1963-1971 (Long)
Mercedes-Benz SL & SLC – 107-series 1971-1989 (Long)
Mercedes-Benz SLK – R170 series 1996-2004 (Long)
Mercedes-Benz SLK – R171 series 2004-2011 (Long)
Mercedes-Benz W123-series – All models 1976 to 1986 (Long)
Mercedes G-Wagen (Long)
MGA (Price Williams)
MGB & MGB GT– Expert Guide (Auto-doc Series) (Williams)
MGB Electrical Systems Updated & Revised Edition (Astley)
Mini Cooper – The Real Thing! (Tipler)
Mini Minor to Asia Minor (West)
Mitsubishi Lancer Evo, The Road Car & WRC Story (Long)
Montlhéry, The Story of the Paris Autodrome (Boddy)
Morgan Maverick (Lawrence)
Morgan 3 Wheeler – back to the future!, The (Dron)
Morris Minor, 60 Years on the Road (Newell)
Moto Guzzi Sport & Le Mans Bible, The (Falloon)
Motor Movies – The Posters! (Veysey)
Motor Racing – Reflections of a Lost Era (Carter)
Motor Racing – The Pursuit of Victory 1930-1962 (Carter)
Motor Racing – The Pursuit of Victory 1963-1972 (Wyatt/Sears)
Motor Racing Heroes – The Stories of 100 Greats (Newman)
Motorsport In colour, 1950s (Wainwright)
MV Agusta Fours, The book of the classic (Falloon)
N.A.R.T. – A concise history of the North American Racing Team 1957 to 1983 (O'Neil)
Nissan 300ZX & 350Z – The Z-Car Story (Long)
Nissan GT-R Supercar: Born to race (Gorodji)
Northeast American Sports Car Races 1950-1959 (O'Neil)
Nothing Runs – Misadventures in the Classic, Collectable & Exotic Car Biz (Slutsky)
Pass the Theory and Practical Driving Tests (Gibson & Hoole)
Pontiac Firebird – New 3rd Edition (Cranswick)
Porsche Boxster (Long)
Porsche 356 (2nd Edition) (Long)
Porsche 908 (Födisch, Neßhöver, Roßbach, Schwarz & Roßbach)
Porsche 911 Carrera – The Last of the Evolution (Corlett)
Porsche 911R, RS & RSR, 4th Edition (Starkey)
Porsche 911, The Book of the (Long)
Porsche 911 – The Definitive History 2004-2012 (Long)
Porsche – The Racing 914s (Smith)
Porsche 911SC 'Super Carrera' – The Essential Companion (Streather)
Porsche 914 & 914-6: The Definitive History of the Road & Competition Cars (Long)
Porsche 924 (Long)
The Porsche 924 Carreras – evolution to excellence (Smith)
Porsche 928 (Long)
Porsche 944 (Long)
Porsche 964, 993 & 996 Data Plate Code Breaker (Streather)
Porsche 993 'King Of Porsche' – The Essential Companion (Streather)
Porsche 996 'Supreme Porsche' – The Essential Companion (Streather)
Porsche 997 2004-2012 – Porsche Excellence (Streather)
Porsche Racing Cars – 1953 to 1975 (Long)
Porsche Racing Cars – 1976 to 2005 (Long)
Porsche – The Rally Story (Meredith)
Porsche: Three Generations of Genius (Meredith)
Preston Tucker & Others (Linde)
RAC Rally Action! (Gardiner)
Racing Colours – Motor Racing Compositions 1908-2009 (Newman)
Rallye Sport Fords: The Inside Story (Moreton)
Renewable Energy Home Handbook, The (Porter)
Roads with a View – England's greatest views and how to find them by road (Corfield)
Rolls-Royce Silver Shadow/Bentley T Series Corniche & Camargue – Revised & Enlarged Edition (Bobbitt)
Rolls-Royce Silver Spirit, Silver Spur & Bentley Mulsanne 2nd Edition (Bobbitt)
Rootes Cars of the 50s, 60s & 70s – Hillman, Humber, Singer, Sunbeam & Talbot (Rowe)
Rover P4 (Bobbitt)
Runways & Racers (O'Neil)
RX-7 – Mazda's Rotary Engine Sportscar (Updated & Revised New Edition) (Long)
Singer Story: Cars, Commercial Vehicles, Bicycles & Motorcycle (Atkinson)
Sleeping Beauties USA – abandoned classic cars & trucks (Marek)
SM – Citroën's Maserati-engined Supercar (Long & Claverol)
Standard Motor Company, The Book of the (Robson)
Steve Hole's Kit Car Cornucopia – Cars, Companies, Stories, Facts & Figures: the UK's kit car scene since 1949 (Hole)
Subaru Impreza: The Road Car And WRC Story (Long)
Supercar, How to Build your own (Thompson)
Tales from the Toolbox (Oliver)
Tatra – The Legacy of Hans Ledwinka, Updated & Enlarged Collector's Edition of 1500 copies (Margolius & Henry)
Taxi! The Story of the 'London' Taxicab (Bobbitt)
To Boldly Go – twenty six vehicle designs that dared to be different (Hull)
Toleman Story, The (Hilton)
Toyota Celica & Supra, The Book of Toyota's Sports Coupés (Long)
Toyota MR2 Coupés & Spyders (Long)
Triumph TR6 (Kimberley)
Two Summers – The Mercedes-Benz W196R Racing Car (Ackerson)
TWR Story, The – Group A (Hughes & Scott)
Unraced (Collins)
Volkswagens of the World (Glen)
VW Beetle Cabriolet – The full story of the convertible Beetle (Bobbitt)
VW Beetle – The Car of the 20th Century (Copping)
VW Bus – 40 Years of Splitties, Bays & Wedges (Copping)
VW Bus Book, The (Bobbitt)
VW Golf: Five Generations of Fun (Copping & Cservenka)
VW – The Air-cooled Era (Copping)
Volkswagen Type 3, The book of the – Concept, Design, International Production Models & Development (Glen)
You & Your Jaguar XK8/XKR – Buying, Enjoying, Maintaining, Modifying – New Edition (Thorley)
Which Oil? – Choosing the right oils & greases for your antique, vintage, veteran, classic or collector car (Michell)
Works Minis, The Last (Purves & Brenchley)
Works Rally Mechanic (Moylan)

Veloce Publishing's other imprints:

BATTLE CRY!

Hubble & Hattie

www.veloce.co.uk

Apps – Download now from www.digital.veloce.co.uk

eBook – Download now from www.digital.veloce.co.uk

For post publication news, updates and amendments relating to this book please visit www.veloce.co.uk/books/V4994

First published in 2005 by Veloce Publishing Limited, Veloce House, Parkway Farm Business Park, Middle Farm Way, Poundbury, Dorchester DT1 3AR, England. Fax 01305 268864 / e-mail info@veloce.co.uk / web www.veloce.co.uk or www.velocebooks.com. Reprinted July 2016 and October 2016. ISBN 978-1-845849-94-8; UPC: 6-36847-04994-2.

© 2005 and 2016 Marcus Chambers, Stuart Turner, Peter Browning and Veloce Publishing. All rights reserved. With the exception of quoting brief passages for the purpose of review, no part of this publication may be recorded, reproduced or transmitted by any means, including photocopying, without the written permission of Veloce Publishing Ltd. Throughout this book logos, model names and designations, etc, have been used for the purposes of identification, illustration and decoration. Such names are the property of the trademark holder as this is not an official publication. Readers with ideas for automotive books, or books on other transport or related hobby subjects, are invited to write to the editorial director of Veloce Publishing at the above address.

British Library Cataloguing in Publication Data – A catalogue record for this book is available from the British Library. Typesetting, design and page make-up all by Veloce Publishing Ltd on Apple Mac. Printed and bound by CPI Group (UK) Ltd, Croydon, CR0 4YY.

BMC COMPETITIONS DEPARTMENT SECRETS

Revealed by managers:
Marcus Chambers
Stuart Turner
Peter Browning

VELOCE PUBLISHING
THE PUBLISHER OF FINE AUTOMOTIVE BOOKS

Contents

INTRODUCTION & ACKNOWLEDGEMENTS.....................5

PART 1   1955-1961
    MARCUS CHAMBERS...............................6

PART 2   1961-1967
    STUART TURNER..................................59

PART 3   1967-1970
    PETER BROWNING...............................138

PART 4   1970-1980
    POSTSCRIPT.....................................181

PART 5
    ROLL OF HONOUR.............................184

OTHER BOOKS BY THE SAME AUTHORS.....................186

INDEX...190

Introduction & Acknowledgements

Many books have been written about the exploits of the BMC Competitions Department. This one is slightly different because in it we take a look behind the scenes, using many documents which, to our knowledge, have never before appeared in print. These give an indication of how the Department functioned within BMC and later Leyland, and help explain the policies – and sometimes politics – of those days.

We discussed at length whether some of the documents should be included because they may not fit with the starry-eyed view sometimes held of those days, but decided that to 'publish and be damned' was the only way to portray a complete and honest picture. Anyway, it was all a very long time ago!

The book could not have been written without the help of Philip Young who convinced three somewhat reluctant authors that they should go ahead, and then bullied us until we did.

Above all, the book could not have been written without the efforts of all the drivers and people in the team at Abingdon; it is to them that this book is dedicated with our grateful thanks.

Marcus Chambers*
Stuart Turner
Peter Browning

* Marcus Chambers passed away at the age of 98 in 2009.

1955-1961

FOUNDATION STONES

MARCUS CHAMBERS

I arrived at Abingdon after talking to former Bentley boy S. C. H. 'Sammy' Davis, who had been brought in as a consultant by MG's General Manager, John Thornley, to advise on returning the factory to front line motorsport. Sammy gave me the tip that John Thornley was seeking help. I'd returned home after working for the Overseas Food Corporation on the peanut producing scheme that had been set up by the British government in Tanganyika, and a spell in British Honduras as estate manager for the Colonial Development Corporation.

My motorsport experience included a couple of drives in HRGs at Le Mans, with a class win in 1939. When World War 2 came to an end, I found myself acting as paid professional team manager for the 1947-48 seasons, helping two wealthy privateers with their new HRG Streamliners. So I'd had experience as a driver as well as a team administrator, and knew my way round regulations, as well as the Continent; the sort of background Sammy Davis presumably thought MG was looking for. I was free to start work immediately and was not tied by family commitments. The letter which Sammy Davis suggested I send to John Thornley must have arrived at the right time ...

The desire to get BMC into motorsport was primarily driven by the Austin management – MG was already committed to the 24 hours of Le Mans with prototype MGAs. At the meeting in December 1954 to formally establish setting up a new BMC Competitions Department, and disband the existing Nuffield Competitions Committee, a general mood of improving confidence prevailed because post war problems – such as steel shortage and rationing – were beginning to fade. An aura of hope pervaded a corporation that was coming to terms with welding together Austin and Nuffield's Morris, MG, Riley and Wolseley.

Meanwhile, up the road in Coventry, Triumph was also planning a factory-based motorsport department. The Triumph TR2 was proving successful in the sportscar market, and Triumph needed to build on the motorsport potential already being exploited by privateers; the car had won the RAC Rally, for example. Triumph's bosses, also meeting in December 1954, decided to form a new department headed by Ken Richardson, fresh from the BRM Formula One team. Triumph and BMC were to become keen rivals.

As if that wasn't enough, Rootes had been quick to return to motorsport, employing Grand Prix drivers like Mike Hawthorn, Peter Collins and Stirling Moss (who took three Alpine Cups in succession to become one of only five drivers to win a Gold Cup). Rootes also had a lighter and more agile Alpine coming on stream and a Sunbeam version of the Minx saloon with disc brakes and an overdrive gearbox.

Three British factories were about to go head-to-head, as well as try and take on Continental teams and drivers on their home ground.

There seemed no time to lose as John Thornley showed me round the Abingdon factory. Factory tours with him were a breathless affair; you

1955 to 1961: FOUNDATION STONES by Marcus Chambers

walked through door after door, with John shouting out peoples' first names which you had to try and remember, all at breakneck speed. Here was Cecil Cousins, now works manager, but who, 25 years before, had driven an M-Type Midget at Brooklands; there was Reg Jackson, now Chief Inspector in charge of quality but another name from motorsport's past. In the Development Department, Alec Hounslow was in charge of building the lightweight MGAs for Le Mans. Alec had been the riding mechanic alongside Nuvolari when he won the TT in a K3 Magnette back in '33. Finally, John introduced me to Syd Enever, designer, and the man who had built record breakers which held more international speed records than any other make in the world. It was a heady introductory tour!

New buildings were being added at the MG factory, and I settled into a small office next door to the Development Department. A few months later, a workshop at the other end of the complex – which had been used to build military vehicles during the war – became available for the exclusive use of the newly titled 'British Motor Corporation Competitions Department'.

The 1955 Monte Carlo Rally was about to start but I had little opportunity to influence our efforts in this – it had already been decided that the MG Car Club could find the right drivers; John Thornley knew most of the drivers personally. There would be three Abingdon-prepared Magnettes, and three Austin Westminsters prepared at Longbridge, so the two wings of the BMC Competitions Committee could feel satisfied. Servicing two very different types of car on the event was not going to be a problem as no on-event servicing was to be allowed. The Committee had insisted that any Austin entry would be prepared at Longbridge, and MG at Abingdon. Only if Longbridge felt overloaded with work pressures would an Austin be prepared at Abingdon. Such territorial 'discussions' were inevitable with a new department representing so many different makes.

The 'Three Musketeers' of Magnettes, along with the Austin Westminsters, started from Glasgow. It was soon obvious that the Magnettes suffered from too much weight; they had to have three-man crews, with all their baggage for a week's rallying that was run virtually without rest. The MGs also had poor traction, and the Austins were equally afflicted. The tail-happy MGs received some first aid at Caffyn's dealership in Ashford on the final run to Dover, when the string binding of the rear springs was cut to allow more movement. (The route down the A20 went through Ashford's town centre and past the Caffyn's showroom. Photographs of the tired and anxious-looking crews, clad in duffel coats and drinking mugs of tea, apparently graced the walls of the office of Caffyn's sales manager for many years after.)

The best result achieved on the '55 Monte was 68th overall for one of the Austins, driven by Mrs 'Bill' Wisdom (wife of leading motoring journalist Tommy Wisdom) who had raced and rallied extensively before the war, navigated by Mrs Joan Johns, who was also experienced. Their names would figure again in team cars under my management but, with the exception of a couple of the MG navigators, including a young Willy Cave who had won the London Rally only a few months earlier in a TR2, I was not at all impressed with the drivers.

I had had these drivers imposed on me. The Tulip was coming up and I could not make immediate changes but I vowed that this would be the last time the crews were not chosen by me. They were fine if you wanted someone to wheel a car round a pylon at the end of Blackpool seafront; the MG Car Club's choice was based purely on this very individual style of British club event, but this bore little relation to driving long distances over mountain passes covered in snow and ice. The drivers were all pretty hopeless, really, and although rather out of their depth, should, and could, have done a lot better. I told John Thornley I thought the Monte was rather a disaster.

The Department had been given a budget of £100,000. It was a fantastic sum (the equivalent of over £2 million in 2016) and it meant that money would never be a problem. In 1955, funds were bolstered further with sponsorship of £10,000 from Castrol.

However, finding experienced, hungry-to-win drivers was not as easy as it is today because all of the drivers I rated were loyal to existing factory drives; drivers didn't flit about from team to team so my only option was to build my own squad. It would have been unthinkable to go and buy the services of a winning driver from the Continent ... after all we were the British Motor Corporation, which surely meant British cars, prepared by British mechanics, and driven by British drivers. We were trying to beat the bloody foreigners ... not send them pay cheques!

It was natural, therefore, that I should turn to those I'd met and trusted through my HRG days. Enter John Gott, then Chief Superintendent of Hertford Constabulary (and soon to be promoted to Chief Constable of Northamptonshire). John had driven in the HRG team before the war, had tackled the RAC Rally in a Frazer Nash, and came with well-rounded experience, and some firm ideas about how things should be done, particularly on the planning and preparation side of things. John had just returned from the Monte Carlo Rally driving one of Ken Richardson's works Standard Tens, and liked the team as well as the car, so persuading him to move to BMC not only gained us someone whose experience we could trust, but deprived Standard of a good British driver at the same time. I was keen to put my stamp on matters, and having the right driving team seemed crucial as I set about building up the Department.

Early in 1955, I acquired a new recruit who could perhaps generate some publicity but who was totally untried, with no previous experience at all. It was Pat Moss and she arrived almost by accident.

Pat had longed for a Triumph TR2, and, having persuaded her father to buy back a share in her horse, finally got hold of her first sportscar ... and decided to enter some club events. An approach to the Coventry factory's Competitions Department elicited the response that it would be willing to lend her a car, even though she had no proven ability or past experience, but not contribute to her expenses. Pat already had a car – it was someone else to pay the expenses that she wanted. And that is how Triumph allowed Stirling's sister to slip through its fingers.

Pat was to play a very significant role in developing the BMC Competitions Department. The rosettes Pat had in her stable from her equine activities actually played a part in the creation of the team's badge. Some of the Continentals used the word 'Ecurie' for a rally team; MG used 'Safety Fast' as a slogan. We were the British Motor Corporation and our badge would have to be tricolour; I got the MG Drawing Office to do an Ecurie Safety Fast layout, based on Pat's showjumping rosettes, and Publicity ordered the stick-on transfers.

After the Monte, we had little over a month to prepare for our next big event, the 1955 RAC Rally, then run in March. The Publicity Department liked the idea of Stirling Moss' sister driving for the new team, and a red MG TF was hastily put together; Pat recalls it would be too generous to say it was 'prepared' as it came without a heater, and no additional foglights "like everyone else", but she was far too polite to point out its shortcomings.

The MG Car Club's Monte drivers were also to be entered again in the 'Three Musketeers of Magnettes', plus a pair of Austin Westminsters with new drivers. At the last minute I was able to get Ian Appleyard – perhaps the most famous British rally driver of that time, and certainly the most successful – on board. Ian had achieved outstanding results with works Jaguar XK120s, and, in fact, set all the best times on the RAC Rally in the previous year. But with the emphasis switching from punch between corners to agility around cones and nimble handling, Ian now reckoned a smaller car with less power could do well ... and fancied an MG YB. I talked him out of that and found another TF, in which Mr and Mrs Appleyard finished eight overall. Triumph's Competitions Department cleaned up with the Standard Ten, finishing first and third, using some BMC bits to make them go, including twin SU carburettors. This sort of thing was considered 'not cricket' and the point was made to the motoring press that Standard was only able to win the rally by using BMC bits. Many years later, Ken Richardson revealed that it was not just carburettors he had pinched – the works Standard Tens ran at their best when fitted with Austin A35 pistons.

Ian Appleyard's eighth proved to me what I'd known all along: even if a car is underpowered and outclassed, the right driver can make an enormous difference. Appleyard took the same car to the Circuit of Ireland the next month and finished fourth overall.

In the spring of 1955, the four Le Mans cars were revealed; codenamed EX182, the EX stood for experimental.

1955 to 1961: FOUNDATION STONES by Marcus Chambers

The model was essentially a lightweight MGA with alloy panels and a lighter chassis, and streamlined open bodywork painted mid-green. The four could not qualify in time as production cars due to the late arrival at Abingdon of body press equipment. In April, Dick Jacobs and Ken Wharton were lined up as test drivers for a session with these cars at Silverstone. John Thornley brought in Sammy Davis as Team Manager, with me as his assistant. I was able to take my wife, Patricia, with me as she was a qualified physiotherapist!

Scrutineering at Le Mans saw much interest in the new MG model, with the French insisting that the exit of the exhaust pipe should be modified, ordering a straight cut-off, instead of it being angled diagonally, so that they did not raise any dust. In the yard of our team hotel Sammy had the drivers practice the Le Mans sprint to the cars.

During practise, the MGs settled into easily beating the 80mph target laps needed to qualify. Arrival of the Triumph TRs – also in green – caused a stir amongst the press; one was to be driven by no less than the team manager himself, Ken Richardson. All were equipped with disc brakes.

Le Mans that year witnessed the worst ever motor racing tragedy when a Mercedes SL driven by Levegh hit the back of Lance Macklin's Healey in front of the pits. The Mercedes planed over the barriers in front of the grandstand and 80 spectators died. Mackin climbed into our MG pit unhurt. The Triumphs and MGs had dug in for a race of attrition. Soon afterward, as smoke rose over the grandstand, Dick Jacobs and MG number 42 went missing ... and another column of smoke rose, this time from White House Corner.

Dick was seriously injured. The previous accident had caused a momentary lapse of concentration, and the MG had hit a bank. After three days in hospital – after his life had been saved by an MG timekeeper who happened to be a doctor – Jacobs was flown home on the personal instruction of BMC Chairman Sir Leonard Lord, but was not discharged from hospital until October.

As for the race, the new MGs had done well, despite the two accidents overshadowing everything. The two surviving MGs finished 12th, and 17th; the best Triumph was 14th, Ken Richardson's TR 15th, and 19th place was taken by a TR2 driven by Morris-Goodall.

The number of deaths of innocent onlookers in the biggest ever motorsport disaster shocked the world. Switzerland, for example, instantly banned all forms of motorsport, despite having its own Grand Prix. One internal BMC memo tried to dispel the gloom with typical stiff upper lip, predicting that motorsport would go on: "For the same reasons ships continue to cross the Atlantic – despite the Titanic". However, there was firm condemnation of the introduction of prototype specialist racers at the expense of production based sportscars, and BMC urged the RAC and others to lobby the organisers to bring about a return to the event's roots.

In the following Ulster TT, two of the Le Mans MGs were entered with experimental twin-cam engines: one designed at great cost by Austin, and the other designed at great cost by Morris Engines; now the rivalry of the two wings of BMC would be made public because the engines were to race against each other. The idea behind this was that the best engine would go into production as a special version of the MGA. (I'd already proposed that a 'GT' Magnette should be built for rallying, with a twin-cam engine, alloy panels, knock-off wheels and a tank with a 300-mile range.) During the TT, two drivers were killed, several cars were involved in accidents, and the press was again filled with gory pictures and headlines containing the word "tragedy".

As a result of this Sir Leonard Lord decreed that our products would be better served if motorsport efforts were concentrated on rallies and record-breaking. The Department now had a clear focus.

John Gott knocked on my door, hinting he might be able to change the driver line-up that was causing me some frustration for some other ex-HRG drivers. Among these was Nancy Mitchell, who had been a member of the Daimler works rally team and won the ladies award on the Alpine in an HRG. I snapped her up for the 1956 season, and by the end of the year she was European Ladies Champion.

With his wide knowledge of MG personnel, John Thornley selected the key figures for the workshop. Dougie Watts – a great judge of men who knew who to select as his fitters – was the foreman; he laid down the rules and didn't tolerate those who broke them.

He had to replace only one of the team in all the time I was there.

Tommy Wellman became Dougie's second in command, in tandem with Doug Hamblin, and the 14-strong team would turn round race and rallycars for the ever-increasing programme of events. Den Green joined the Department in 1958, and Cliff Humphries – who proved something of a genius in engine development – soon after. I was given my own secretary, and, after four years in the job, my own assistant, Bill Price, who went on to play a major role in the future. Drivers receive most of the glory for competition successes but one should never forget the vital roles played by people like Dougie and his team. I once calculated that before I stepped down, almost 300 cars were prepared and entered in international motorsport by this tiny team; in addition, privateers received help and in 1956, for example, no fewer than 59 privateer cars also went through the Competitions Department.

With a six figure budget, it made sense to allocate part to helping talented privateers. John Sprinzel took delivery of an early production 'Frogeye' Sprite with the works number PM0200, which was to grace all manner of rallycars later. The founder of one of Britain's first go-faster tuning shops with modified parts sold as accessories from lock-up garages in Lancaster Mews, John became an occasional member of the rally team, and often accompanied John Gott on recce trips, helping in the preparation of advance team notes, pages of memos, refining navigation, warning of tight sections, where to refuel, and where best to take tyres from Dunlop. The two Johns were very different characters, as John Sprinzel recalled recently:

"It was a gentlemanly swan across Europe. Not on the road at first light, oh no, John Gott would come down to breakfast in his dressing gown, then go back to his room for a bath, and we'd be on the road soon after nine. By 10.30, we would be looking for a coffee-shop, then there would be lunch, and by three we would be wondering if we shouldn't be looking out for somewhere to stay the night. This is how things were done then. Someone as impatient as me found it rather trying but the principles of looking at the state of roads when many of the remoter climbs were in a poor state of repair, and just about all the rallying mountain passes were gravel were sound. The strategy of gaining advance knowledge to beat the foreigners on their home ground was dead right. In some ways we were ahead of the game. We could now begin to pace the cars properly, plan tyres and refuelling in a more professional manner."

I was never entirely free of influence 'from on high'. Every now and then I'd bump into some manager in a corridor who would wag his finger and say "You've not campaigned a Wolseley for a while, Mr Chambers!" It meant I had to walk on eggshells at times, while trying to do things my way. In fairness, I never felt particularly under pressure by management, nobody complained about a lack of outright results, for example, although we were watching what Sunbeam and Triumph were doing. They had a natural winner or two in their locker, and we didn't feel we had that; all the time we were looking forward to things we knew were coming along, like the six-cylinder engine in the Austin Healey. But we were learning and building experience. The Publicity and Advertising Departments were perfectly happy; we gave them lots of copy, and they would book space in advance when we looked like winning a class. A lot of 'success' advertising established an image of various makes and models being top of the class in a variety of events. Some very ordinary cars were given a certain degree of charisma; after all, Monte Carlo was considered far-off and glamorous and an Austin A40 finishing tenth overall on the Monte could be used to good effect by the Publicity Department. Given we had no natural outright winner, achieving something to shout about for a variety of different models made strategic sense.

Although serious about matters we were still able to consider outlandish events. One opportunity came via a begging letter from a bunch of students. The Cambridge University Automobile Club was writing around manufacturers seeking the loan of a small car to have a crack at some long-distance class records. The FIA World Speed Records had a myriad of classes and categories, some of which had not been contested for some time, and the proposal was for an Austin A35 to run for a week, flat out. The students were at pains to stress that this was a works

1955 to 1961: FOUNDATION STONES by Marcus Chambers

entry; all they wanted was the loan of a prepared car as all the work of hiring the circuit and running the team would be done by them. We had little to lose – the fact that they were students lent greater credence to publicity opportunities. The letter arrived when the Department was short of events. The Suez Crisis had caused the cancellation of several major rallies, like the RAC Rally and Alpine Rally. With a lean year for events, record-breaking could fill in and, in any case, I knew if I turned down the students, they would call up Triumph for a Standard Ten. So an Austin A35 in British Racing Green was found (actually an A30 development car that had been given A35 'upgrades'), and an A35 engine prepared and balanced with a 30mm downdraft Zenith from another Austin model. Other modifications included a 50-litre fuel tank and shock absorbers set 20 per cent harder. The only special component was a 3.9 differential (which went into production many years later, ending up in the 1500cc MG Midget). Harder VG95 brake linings all round were fitted – although the car was not expected to do much braking. Dunlop produced several sets of crossply tyres, the narrowest that would stay on the standard rims, but with a harder rubber compound (lorry rubber); everyone prayed that it wouldn't rain. A few days of workshop time, and Abingdon could now go chasing international land-speed records.

The summer of 1958 was particularly hot, and, as this was a student jaunt, some of the Cambridge supporters decided to ferry a few crates of beer to the banked track at Montlhéry by rubber-rafting down the Loire. When they arrived, they realised that matters were being taken more seriously than they'd expected: there was a Shell tanker, a Dunlop van, our BMC motorsport service bus, and works mechanics in overalls with BMC on the back.

The driver line-up comprised Gyde Horrocks as team leader, Ray Simpson, Arthur Taylor, Tom Threlfall, and Peter Riviere, with pit support from John Aley (later famous for his roll cages) and would-be vicar Rupert Jones acting as pit signallers, lap scorers, radiator de-buggers and windscreen cleaners.

Records began to fall, even though temperatures inside the car were at times at 120 degrees F. The plan was straightforward: ten thousand miles by a baby car in ten thousand minutes, but if the pace could be increased to 75mph, then International Class G records would fall into their laps, providing they could keep going for four days – or more.

The four-day record fell with an average speed of 74.95mph, and that for five days at the same speed, then six days-and-nights ... then, 20,000 kilometres in seven days – all records captured by a margin of 12 per cent. Not bad, for a stunt dreamed up in a Cambridge pub ...

With a bunch of records safely in the bag, I couldn't resist pulling rank and took the wheel for a few laps just as the seven-day record was about to fall, and so my name went into the FIA record books for the first and only time.

The A35's clutch of records stood for a year, and, as testimony to the fact that it was a bright idea, Ford went out and took all the records in a highly modified one-litre Anglia the following year.

By 1959 we had campaigned just about anything and everything in the BMC range. A win at international level had eluded us, although the Austin Healey was now delivering even more power with a full three-litre engine. Then a Mini 850 was delivered to the workshop "for assessment". It stayed in the car park for several days – nobody rushed to drive it. Indeed, Dougie Watts recalled that one lunchtime he needed to pop into town to cash a cheque, and looked around for a car. Dougie walked over to the Mini ... and then changed his mind. He took a Healey instead. The Mini seemed such an insignificant-looking little car. For years we had wanted to get our hands on a rally winner but when it arrived nobody realised that the Mini was the answer to our prayers.

The only way to discover potential was to enter it in an event, which is how I became the first person to rally a Mini, taking a standard car with just a sumpshield and a map light, and doing the Viking Rally of 1959. Pat Moss was already down to drive in 'Alf', her faithful red Austin A40, (947AOF). I nursed the car to the finish, 51st overall, gaining useful experience – with broken wheels, leaky boot and floors, there was much to do to turn the Mini into a proper rallycar.

Everyone said it would never beat the Saab, and it did overtake me often.

11

BMC Competitions Department Secrets ...

There was heather growing up the middle of the stages and those small wheels combined with low ground clearance made it a figure of ridicule for some, but after the Viking Rally I realised it had potential. I thought it would help us climb the learning curve to enter it in a few club rallies, so I asked Pat to take a Morris Mini Minor on the aptly-named Mini-Miglia national rally the following month with Stuart Turner, one of the best club navigators of the day. They finished first overall – with a winning margin of ten minutes. It might only have been a national rally, but the new Mini had won hands down, only second time out.

The RAC Rally was now just weeks away, and a team of three 850 Minis was entered for Pat Ozanne, Ken James and Alec Pitt. This was a gamble on a high profile event that ran for four days all round the UK, and Pat, in fact, preferred to drive the car she called 'Granny', a venerable Morris Minor which simply refused to die.

New signings the Morley brothers were in a works Healey, as was Jack Sears, who had developed the 100/6 into a rallycar, with Willy Cave in a second Austin Healey, and John Williamson and Johnny Milne in a third.

Moving Britain's premier rally to November for the first time was supposed to spice up the show with the uncertainty of bad weather, but nobody could have predicted the chaos a heavy fall of snow would cause in Scotland. Pat got through, with some pushing and shoving from Erik Carlsson, with snowchains on the Minor, to manage only third overall in the Ladies' Category and 26th overall, but the Morleys finished fourth and first in class. The Minis all retired with slipping clutches; way to go, as I think they say nowadays ...

Pat had taken second overall in the summer of 1960 on the Alpine Rally, which clearly suited the long legs of the big Healey. Then the team finally achieved the big breakthrough we'd been working toward with almost a clean sweep on the Liège-Rome-Liège – a punishing 96 hours from Spa across Eastern Europe to Yugoslavia – and back again. Pat and Ann Wisdom won in an Austin Healey, the first time a woman driver had won an international rally, and the first time BMC had claimed first place in Europe. John Sprinzel finished third in a Sprite, new recruits to the team, David Seigle-Morris and Vic Elford finished fifth, with John Gott and Rupert Jones tenth. First in the Ladies, 2nd and 5th in the GT class, and the team prize: at the prizegiving BMC was bursting with pride; so too was Pat, who had to be literally sewn into her party frock by Ann Wisdom after splitting a seam whilst changing. Never mind the 96 hours of driving, the team seemed determined to celebrate for the next 96! Returning home via Paris, I have to confess I took a plaque off the wall of the Crazy Horse nightclub: it's in front of me as I write.

On the German Rally just a few weeks later, David Seigle-Morris and Stuart Turner took the GT category with a big Healey, and the year ended with strong performances from Healey drivers on the RAC Rally.

More to the point, the Minis were now showing undeniable promise. David Seigle-Morris finished 6th overall on the RAC in a Mini 850, the Mini's best international result so far, and Mike Sutcliffe and Derek Astle came eighth.

We now had what we wanted – the Austin Healey 3000, rugged, simple and with 200bhp capable of outgunning most of the opposition, and the Mini clearly showing potential for anything twisty with a premium on handling.

But although matters looked bright, after seven years I felt that writing the next chapter was best handed over to someone else. My personal diary of 1961 shows that I was restless and eager for a change. I sounded out John Thornley to see if maybe a move to the Publicity Department or similar could be found, but was stonewalled. I felt I had no choice but to resign and take up an offer from an old friend who had helped me right at the outset by delivering the team's first significant result, Ian Appleyard. In my present position I was away from my wife and two young children for a lot of the time, as well as an elder son who was at public school, so the offer from Ian came at the right time. It meant a move to Yorkshire to become service manager of a BMC dealership. I was still involved with cars and motoring but could now have much more of a homelife.

I recognised that rallying was changing, and we needed to change, but, frankly, after seven years I was feeling in a bit of a rut. If the team was to make the best of its potential – and we were under mounting pressure to deliver more wins – it was best if

1955 to 1961: FOUNDATION STONES by Marcus Chambers

someone else took the helm. After a successful year in 1961, going out with the team in winning form at what seemed a peak also seemed a sound move. In talks with John Thornley, David Seigle-Morris was considered for my job. He was someone who could put on a tie and walk into a boardroom and win an argument without having to thump the table. Thornley liked his manner; working in London's County Hall had perhaps given him an insight into political footwork, and he certainly knew his motorsport. But, I also knew he enjoyed competing, hungered after an Alpine Cup, and I doubted he would drive a desk.

I had other ideas about who should have the position. It would be someone very much younger than the rest of us, someone who had been around motorsport. It would be a big leap of faith but I told Thornley he should go head-hunting for a young reporter on *Motoring News* called Stuart Turner.

A new era for the BMC Competitions Department was about to begin ....

```
13.12.54

Formation of BMC Competitions Committee

Meeting held at Longbridge to consider directive from Mr Harriman that BMC got
to the top in competitions and that the necessary money to achieve this would
be made available.

The present Nuffield Comptition Committee be dissolved and a new one set up
based at Abingdon. It would consist of the General Manager of the Abingdon
factory as Chairman, one representative from Austin and one from Nuffield
plus the BMC Central Publicity Manager.

This Committee would be empowered (except as provided below) to enter any BMC
product, including Austin Healey, in any competition which it thought fit, or
to assist private owners of such products to do so. The exceptions were:
            a) The MG programme already agreed.
            b) The racing activities of the Donald Healey Motor Co.

Austin cars would be prepared in the Experimental Shop at Longbridge. All
others would be prepared at Abingdon. (Mr Palmer added a rider that he was
anxious that the Experimental Shop at Longbridge should not be flooded. It was
agreed therefore that work beyond the capacity of this shop be done at
Abingdon).

The tentative ceiling expenditure within the control of the Competitions
Committee was agreed at £100,000. This sum to be split between Austin and
Nuffield. Mr E.H.Goddard to be asked to suggest method of accounting.
```

The start of it all. The tentative budget was substantial in those days.

```
4.1.55
Mr Harriman agrees to the nomination of M.Chambers to the Committee. The
other members:
R.W.Grice   Chief Road Test Superintendent, A.M.Co Longbridge, Mr R.A.Bishop
BMC Central Publicity Manager and J.W.Thornley.
```

When I joined the Competitions Committee in January 1955 it was still small – always a good thing.

1955 to 1961: FOUNDATION STONES by Marcus Chambers

13.1.55

Competition Committee Meeting

Special series of cars:

    a) Which cars currently available
    b) Which are the suitable events
    c) Which form basis for future development

The most promising cars considered were:

    Austin Healey   A90 Westminster 6/90 Wolseley
    Austin Healey 100S 4/44 Wolseley   Riley Pathfinder
                                                 MG Magnette
                                                 MGTF 1500

The MGA 1500 already enters for Le Manstto replace the TF in June.

Later the Austin Healey to take the A90-6 engine.
The twin cam was spoken of and is supposed to be available in 1956.

The new competition shop would not be available until April 1, 1955.

Agreed that all work for competitions be carried out at Abingdon.

An idea specification for the Magnette using twin cam engine and disc brakes was submitted with close ratio gears and knock off wheels, with 300-mile fuel tank.

Almost too many cars from which to choose, but no potential outright winner.

Review of position: Mid-Feb 1955

Monte Carlo Rally

3 Austin Westminsters   3 Magnettes
Best finisher: Mrs Wisdom, Austin. 68th General Classification
5th Ladies, starting from Lisbon

The MGs already suffering from poor power-to-weight ratio carried too much gear. Glasgow starters had a poor run. The Magnettes suffered from indifferent roadholding. The MGs had been fitted with an extra leaf in each rear spring and the springs were lagged with cord. The consequent reduction in roll caused the cars to be very tail happy on black ice. The weather conditions in the recce Dec 26-31 failed to show up this fault. In the rally the binding was removed at Ashford but the rear suspension was still too stiff.

The Westminsters displayed no real vice but rather lacked adhesion at the rear; traction on ice and packed snow was not good.

RAC Rally

Entries made for 3 Westminsters. Mr and Mrs Fotheringham Parker Mr. and Mrs John, Mr and Mrs J.J. Aigun. 3 TFs to be driven by experienced members of MG Car Club. The three Monte Magnettes with the same crews.

Pat Moss running a fourth TF for the ladies prize: If she shapes up well, we will use her more widely and train her for rally work, particularly in view of the good reflected publicity.

Ian Appleyard has elected to run an MG YB saloon but may switch to an MG TF.

As the date on this document indicates, a flurry of activity accompanied the Department set up. Although "the good reflected publicity" was a reference to Pat's brother, Stirling, who was – and still is, of course, a household name – Pat quickly became famous in her own right. The mark of a quick driver is when other drivers look at their stage times, they soon began to study Pat's.

```
8 March 1955

Meeting of Competitions Committee

Approval of a limited number of Westminsters with high-performance
engines.
Also a twin cam 6 cyl later
Accent to be on gaining experience for the Department.
AH 100 for Lance Macklin, Le Mans. Contracts Castrol and Shell

Record attempt:

In anticipation of the proven outputs available from the new
twin cam OHC 1½ litre and after wind tunnel tests of 1/8th scale
models in the high speed wind tunnel at Armstrong-Whitworths at
Baginton had shown that 250 mph was within reach.
Stirling Moss had been approached and a tentative date of
August 1957 made. The reason for approaching Stirling was not
only for his top publicity value but his size which with the
car tailored to fit him might save as much as 20 or 30 HP.

Healey might like to go if approval was given for the record
attempt.

Approval was sought to use a BMC heading as it was not right
to use MG paper when dealing with Austin matters.
```

Back then, record-breaking was taken very seriously. As the final minute makes clear, minor 'political' issues were slowly being sorted out.

<u>IN DESPERATION</u>

From: M. Chambers
To: Mr. J.W. Thornley

October 6 1955

Normal Series Production Cars

At the present time, we have only one car which falls in this category which might make some sort of showing in very minor events abroad and the two British International Rallies. Namely the MG ZA Magnette. No other car in the BMC range stands any chance of success at all.

We are in desperate need of a first class Rally car in the Normal Series Production Class, as until one is manufactured we must continue to run in the Special Series. This will automatically exclude us from the Touring Car Championship and the Ladies Championship.

I would therefore suggest that it is of some importance to consider the possibility of cataloguing a special A90 and a special MG Magnette.

Marcus Chambers
Competitions Manager

The cry of competition managers throughout the ages – more power, please! This memo followed appraisals of all the cars in the current BMC line-up.

27.6.55.

LE MANS 1955.

PERFORMANCE.

As tests at Silverstone had shown that a sustained lap speed of 85 m.p.h. and a maximum lap speed of 94 m.p.h. were theoretically possible, it was particularly gratifying to note that Car No.41 driven by Miles-Lockett averaged 86.78 m.p.h. (Motor figures) or 86.93 m.p.h. (French newspapers). These figures are subject to official confirmation as there is an adjustment to be made for the cars actual time past the finishing line at the end of the race.

The fastest lap also by No. 41 (Miles/Lockett) was made at 93.729 m.p.h. The second car No.42 (Jacobs/Flynn) suffered an unfortunate accident in its 28th lap at White House Corner. As no other cars were involved and nothing has been found to indicate mechanical failure, it can only be attributed to an error of judgment on the part of Jacobs. He had acknowledged a slow-down signal on the completion of his previous lap.

The third car, which had been in reserve, was admitted by the organisers the day before the race. This was No. 64 (Lund/Waeffler). The Competitions Manager decided that the car should be kept just above the qualifying speed and every effort should be made for the car to finish when the second car went out. The drivers of this car were not of the same calibre as those in No.41 and nothing spectacular was expected of them. Lund committed an error of judgment on Lap 175 at about 9.05 a.m. on Sunday morning and rammed a ditched Jaguar, bending his frame and damaging the left front wing and head lamp and putting the front wheels 1¼" out of track. The car remained drivable and qualified 40 minutes before the end of the race. His average speed for the race was 81.6 m.p.h. No attempt was made to improve positions in the race or class at any time as the object of the operation was to qualify for the Bi-annual Cup.

It is of interest to note that No.41's speed for the race was faster than that of the winning Ferrari driven by L.Chinetti in 1949.

It is also a fact that, with the exception of the Triumphs, the M.G.s more closely resembled a production car than any other in the race. Much favourable comment was heard on the fact that the cars were driven back from the race.

PIT PERSONNEL.

With very minor exceptions, which are included in a more detailed report, all those who went over with the team pulled their weight.

Recommendations for next year and subsequent events are contained in that Report. S.C.H.Davis, Stan. Nicholls (Timekeeper) and Dr. M. King are particularly to be congratulated on fine work.

DRIVERS.

We shall need first rank drivers in the future but there is no reason why we should not retain Miles and Lockett who were driving well within their capabilities.

2.

TRANSPORTER.

This vehicle fulfilled its functions well but minor alterations are desirable. A Diesel engined chassis might have been an improvement from the fuel consumption point of view. The average was 10 m.p.g.

MEDICAL AID.

It was more than provident that we had with us Dr. M. King who was acting as a Chartkeeper. According to Dr. Pile of the Churchill he undoubtedly saved R. Jacobs' life, but it must be placed on record that it was only by good luck that Dr.White had an up-to-date passport and was able to raise an emergency team who had passports. Dr.White says he will see that his staff keep their passports up-to-date, and it is incumbent on the Competitions Manager to keep Dr.White informed of the whereabouts of racing teams when abroad.

RACE REPORTS.

Due to the Mercedes accident, communication with England after the race and for several days was not easy. Longer telegrams from Le Mans would no doubt have put Cowley in the picture and possibly have prevented the false report which appeared in the Monday "Evening Standard" to the effect that Jacobs was dead. It is felt that if we are to get the news through efficiently, we should have a member of Publicity on the team.

MERCEDES ACCIDENT.

As a result of the accident, the form of next year's race is most likely to be changed, and there is no reason why we should not take steps, through the R.A.C. and other channels, to see that the race is run on lines which suit us and other British Manufacturers.

If we look back to the early years of this race, it will be remembered that it was for standard production models to which minor modifications were permitted. This category still remains in the race, but the introduction of the prototype has almost eliminated the Standard Production Sports car and it is at present impossible to win the race or a class except with a prototype. In the opinion of the Competitions Manager, prototypes should be excluded, but bodies which conform to the F.I.A. rules should be permitted together with the permitted modifications to the chassis. I think the race would regain some of its past value, and one off jobs such as the Nardi would make way for some serious entries and permit the return of some of the private entries which have now been almost excluded.

Concerning the accident itself, no doubt the competent authority will make a pronouncement in due course, but whilst it is to be deplored, it should be realised that it was brought about by a chain of circumstances which might never occur again in a lifetime. Motor racing will go on for the same reason that ships still cross the Atlantic although the Titanic is no more.

A memo circulated by John Thornley after the ill-fated 1955 Le Mans race. The accident involving Dick Jacobs led to better plans for medical cover for the team – see MEDICAL AID. No progress was made with attempts to restrict the race to standard production models.

BMC Competitions Department Secrets ...

CONDENSED REPORT ON COMPETITION DEPARTMENT'S
CONTINENTAL TEST, 3RD/13TH JULY 1955.

OBJECT. The cancellation of the Alpine Rally deprived us of essential experience on the MGA. prototype. It was therefore decided to utilise available shipping and hotel bookings to test under Alpine conditions not only Ex.182, but also a production MGA., and various other cars in rally trim.

CARS TAKEN.
1. Austin Westminster, with tuned single carburetter engine, lowered rear springs, high rate front springs, and 4.1 axle.

2. Austin Cambridge, fitted with Le Mans engine, complete with oil cooler, E.242 brake linings, Michelin X tyres, and with battery fitted aft.

3. M.G. Magnette, as used in Silverstone Production Car Race, i.e. with Le Mans engine.

4. M.G. Ex.182, as prepared for Alpine Trial.

5. MGA, production car, standard in all respects.

PERSONNEL.
A.S. Enever.
M. Chambers.
A. Hounslow.
D. Watts.
} B.M.C.

J. Milne.
W. Shepherd.
G. Gibson.
J. Williamson.
} Alpine drivers.

H. Keller.
H. Zweifel.
} Alpine drivers. (Swiss, part-time)

PROGRAMME.
Sunday, 3rd July. Abingdon - Le Touquet.
Monday, 4th " Le Touquet - Adenau.
Tuesday, 5th " Nurburgring - Testing.
Wednesday, 6th " Adenau - Wittel.
Thursday, 7th " Wittel - Col de la Faucille - Geneva.
Friday, 8th " Geneva - Col des Aravis, Col du Marais, Col des Essereiux, Col de Tamie, Col de la Forclaz - Talloires.
Saturday, 9th " Col de l'Iseran, Col du Gallibier, Col du Lautaret, Col du Glandon, Col de la Croix de Fer, Col de la Forclaz.
Sunday, 10th " Check cars. Rest.
Monday, 11th " Talloires - Etampes.
Tuesday, 12th " Montlhery - Testing.
Wednesday, 13th " Etampes - Abingdon.

Total mileage, average - 2300.

BRIEF CAR REPORTS.

1. Westminster. This car was taken primarily as baggage and spares car. The general reliability was good and the maintenance of engine tune impressive.

The 4.1 axle appeared to be about ideal.

The suspension still left something to be desired.

The steering column gear control proved to be very indefinite when attempting snap changes under Alpine conditions. Cars will in future be fitted with central control on the floor.

-2-

In attempting to maintain speeds as scheduled for the Alpine Trials in the mountains, brakes failed through fluid vaporisation. Drums are to be ventilated as on Le Mans cars.

2. Cambridge. This was delivered to Abingdon two days before departure. A Le Mans engine was installed and E.242 brake linings fitted, but no other alterations made. The performance was most impressive and confirmed our view that this car is a potential rally winner. As on the Westminster, the brake fluid vaporised towards the end of Saturday, 9th July. Condition of the linings and drums is, however, satisfactory. Drums are to be ventilated as on Le Mans cars.

The engagement of 2nd gear from 3rd in fast mountain descents was a hazardous operation. The car is to be fitted with a Magnette gear control fitted backwards until such time as the centre control being prepared for Australia is available.

Suspension and damping needs substantial stiffening for rally work.

Trouble was experienced with the flexible oil pipes (Super-flexit) to the oil cooler, and this eliminated the car from the test at Montlhery. Super-flexit pipes have in the past been extensively used by M.G. without trouble. It is thought that this present trouble may be due to use of Castrol R. with the current additives. The whole subject is being pursued with the manufacturers, and with two alternative suppliers.

Seating needs attention for rally use, bucket seats being desirable.

Gearbox ratios are too wide for optimum performance. Magnette ratios are to be fitted, together with 4.55 axle.

The Michelin X tyres proved to be very satisfactory indeed. There was little discernible difference in the lap times at Nurburg wet or dry. The total wear for the entire trip was 1.5 mm., as compared with an average of 2.5 mm. on standard Dunlop and 6 mm. on the Dunlop racing. The tyre was much quieter in operation than either of the other two.

3. Magnette. This car also had trouble with flexible oil pipes, but was otherwise trouble free. Rally schedules were easily maintained. Brakes modified as on Le Mans cars and using E.242 linings showed no signs of fade or fluid trouble. The E.242 lining is very good for heavy use of the kind experienced in rallies, but may possibly be regarded as too harsh for production purposes.

4. EX.182. Excessive heat in the driving compartment would have necessitated the removal of the under trays if these cars had run in the actual Alpine Trial. The constriction of the hot air from the engine compartment, and the use of light alloy ramps, floorboards and gearbox cowling, scantily protected with rexine, is responsible for this.

In common with the other cars fitted with the Le Mans type engine, this one suffered from heavy oil consumption, mainly due to the use of 3-ring pistons. Oil leaks from flexible pipes on this car were slight only.

There were sharply divided opinions as to the gearbox ratios, one faction persisting that closer ratios would have improved overall performance in the mountains.

In all other respects the car proved to be ideal for the purpose.

(Page 20-21) A report, written by me but sent out under John Thornley's name, on a major test intended to further explore the competition potential of the range.

1955 to 1961: FOUNDATION STONES by Marcus Chambers

```
                                    -3-

     5.   MGA.  The salient lesson on this car was that the engine
     lost tune at the bottom end towards the end of the trip.    This
     has not yet been accounted for, and is being investigated.

          The gear shift was found to stiffen to an uncomfortable
     degree when hot.  Moreover, reverse and second gear were lost
     completely at Nurburg, and came back of their own accord later.
     Also, the gearbox lost oil.  The gearbox has been removed and
     returned to Mr. Appleby for investigation.

          Brakes - this car was fitted with DM.12 linings as on pro-
     duction.  As was expected, it was found possible to fade the
     linings in the mountains, but there was never any loss of pedal.

          Various items of trim came unstuck in the course of the
     trip, and hood and tonneau fasteners pulled out.  This has been
     referred to Bodies Branch.

TIMES.
              Car.         Nurburg Lap Time.     Montlhery Lap Speed.

              Westminster.       -                    91.25

              Cambridge.      14 mins.                  -

              Magnette.       13 mins. 55 secs.       96.61

              Ex.182.         13 mins. 47 secs.      101.79

              MGA.            14 mins. 19 secs.       96.61 hood & screens.
                                                           Driver only.

                                                      91.3  open.
                                                            2 up.

          Distribution :  (as for Competition Committee Minutes)
                          Sir Leonard Lord, K.B.E.
                          Mr. G.W. Harriman.
                          Mr. R.F. Hanks.
                          Mr. S.V. Smith.
                          Mr. J.R. Edwards.
                          Mr. W.V. Appleby.(4)
                          Mr. G.B. Ashton.
                          Mr. A.S. Enever.
                          Mr. S.V. Haddleton.
                          Mr. E. Maher.

                          Mr. J.W. Thornley.
                          Mr. R.W. Grice.
                          Mr. M. Chambers.
                          Mr. R.A. Bishop.
                          Mr. G. Jones.

JWT/GEVC.
19.7.55.
```

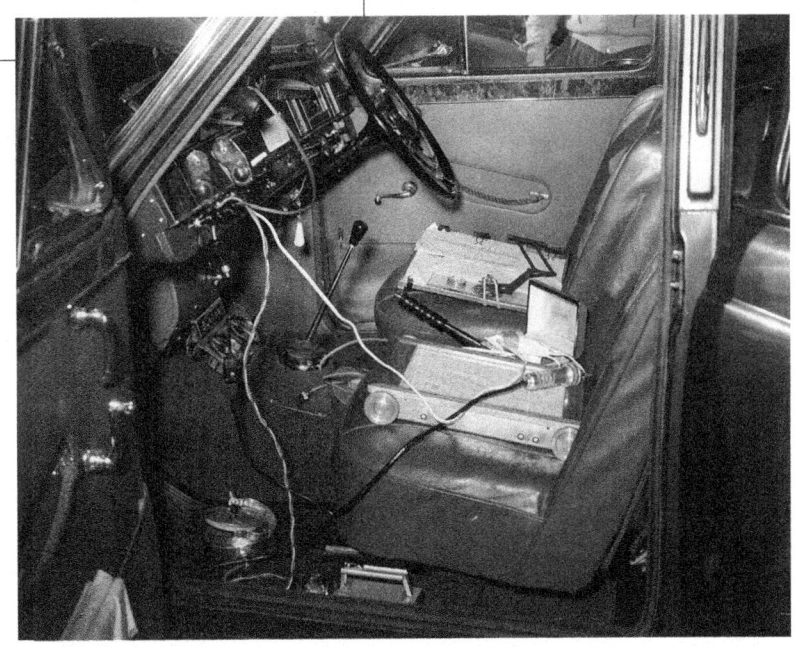

Inside the works MG Magnette. This is the 'office' of Willy Cave for the 1955 Monte Carlo Rally. Note the route instructions contained in a special roller; reminiscent of the device used by Denis Jenkinson to guide Stirling Moss on the Mille Miglia.

REPORT ON TOURIST TROPHY 1955.

It was originally intended to run three cars :

(i) An MGA. fitted with the Morris-Engines-designed 80° twin camshaft engine, and disc brakes.

(ii) An MGA. fitted with the Austin-designed 66° engine, and disc brakes.

(iii) An MGA. in normal Le Mans trim.

Both twin o.h.c. engines were received only very shortly before the cars were due to leave for Belfast, and initial road trials showed that in both cases carburation was unsatisfactory, twin choke Solexes being fitted which starved on corners. Additionally, the maximum r.p.m. of the 66° engine restricted the performance to much the same as that of a standard Le Mans car. It was therefore decided, as there was little prospect of being able to correct both engines in the time available, to substitute a further Le Mans engine for the 66° engine, and to pursue correction of the carburation difficulties on the 80° engine.

Engines Branch, under Mr. Maher, did a sterling job in this connection, and produced a new induction manifold with two twin Weber carburetters in time for these to be flown to Belfast on the Thursday before the race. These were fitted, and the car practised satisfactorily on Friday.

In the race, however, the car, driven by Flockhart/Lockett, was dogged by mis-firing when hot. In its cooler moments it showed a very good turn of speed and lapped at 79.46 m.p.h. Mis-firing persisted and the car was withdrawn at half distance. It was subsequently found to be suffering from a split in the fabricated induction manifold which opened at high temperatures. The performance of the car was, however, extremely promising, and in the absence of this defect would undoubtedly have mixed it with the Porsches.

The second car, i.e. with Le Mans engine and disc brakes, driven by Fairman/Wilson, was reliable and fast, lapped at 77.39 m.p.h., completed the race at 71.07 m.p.h., finished 4th in its class behind 3 Porsches, and ahead of all the works T.R.2s.

The 3rd car, Lund/Stoop, retired on the 8th lap with a split in its experimental alloy fuel tank. This tank had been extensively road-tested, but its failure in the race was undoubtedly attributable to the peculiar conditions. The car "took off" once per lap on 'Deers Leap', and the buffeting of 20 gallons of fuel proved too much for the tank's seams.

JWT/GEVC.
14.10.55.

As this note circulated by John Thornley makes clear, motorsport and mainstream engineering worked closely on important events like the TT.

REPORTS ON RECORDS TAKEN BY
AUSTIN A35
MONTLHERY JULY 1 - 8

Track and conditions

The high speed track was used, running in an anti-clockwise direction. The surface was not as bumpy as we had been lead to believe. The car was driven about 5ft. inside the yellow line. The circuit measures 2.548 kilometres.

The weather was fine for all but the last six hours of the run. Conditions were unusual in so far as the temperature by day and night was unusually high even for July. The average ambient temperature during the day was 90°F and most nights it was around 80°F. The temperatures inside the car during the afternoon varied between 110°F and 120°F. During the last night a squall with winds of up to 40 m.p.h. blew over the track and died down very quickly, and was followed by thunder storms with heavy rain the following morning. The car ran from 3 p.m. July 1st to 3 p.m. July 8th.

Breakdowns and repairs

The offside rear spring shackle plate came loose at one pin and was repaired with a suitable bolt. Spares carried on the car were as follows:-

- 1 Front hub c/w races
- 1 Exhaust valve c/w springs etc.
- 1 Inlet   "   "   "   "
- 1 Set gaskets
- 1 Water pump
- 1 Fan
- 2 Fan belts
- 1 Distributor complete
- 1 Inlet manifold
- 1 Coil
- 4 H/lamp bulbs
- 6 Filter elements
- 2 Rockers
- 2 Push rods
- 1 Top rad hose & clips
- 1 Btm. rad hose & clips
-   Petrol flex pipes
- 1 Std. oil pipe & connections
-   Accel. return spring
-   Spares for Zenith filter
- 1 R/counter cable
- 1 Wiper blade
- 2 Wheel nuts
- 1 Rad cap
-   Locking wire
-   Electric wire
- 1 Box nuts bolts & washers
- 1 Mechanics tool kit
- 1 Set shockers

Equipment - Where it differed from standard.

1. Oil cooler connected with flexible pipes. Capacity with contents of pipes - 1.00 pint.
2. 30 mm. V.I.G. down draught Zenith Carburettor (no air cleaner) Main 95 Comp. 90 Pump 5.0 Choke 27 mm.
3. Zenith petrol filter - commercial type multi-plate
4. Brightray seat exhaust valves. Springs 1D
5. Vandervell thin wall bearings, big ends and mains
6. 50 litre fuel tank with duplicated fuel lines
7. S.U. fuel pump
8. Rear axle ratio 3.90
9. D2/103 Tyres. Dunlop standard tread made in special composition.
10. Dynamo - Lucas high output. (Ball bearings both ends of shaft)
11. Spare coil
12. Specially balanced propeller shaft.
13. Standard shockabsorbers set up 20%

- 2 -

14. 1¼ down pipe to exhaust box.
15. Ferodo VG 95 brake linings
16. Throttle stop (adjustable)
17. Revolution counter
18. Oil gauge, water temp. gauge, ammeter.
19. Accessories

Deleted	Added
Front and rear bumpers	Halda
Side lights	Radio
Heater (added air duct)	Screen washer
Nave plates	Fairing under front bumper

A complete service was carried out every 12 hours and comprised:-

Refuelling
Sump drained and refilled (drained every day at 09.00)
Water topped up if necessary
Filter changed if necessary (twice in run)
Gearbox checked
Rear axle checked
Steering greased
Tyre changes if required
Windscreen and headlamp glasses cleaned
Battery topped up
General examination of car for defects
Flies blown from exterior of radiator core

A routine stop to change drivers comprised:-

Refuelling
Check level in engine
Check radiator level

Engine stripped for examination

When stripped there was no measurable wear anywhere. If the engine had been decarbonised on the 7th day there is no reason why it should not have continued to 14 days. Carbon was masking both valves and caused a slight loss of performance. The exhaust valves needed grinding in. The mixture was certainly on the rich side, as the overall fuel consumption figure works out at 28 m.p.g. All bearings were perfect and were handed to Vandervells for their museum.

Fuel BP super   **Oil** Castrol XL

Drivers
Simpson
Taylor
Threlfall
Horrocks
Riviere
Chambers

Appendix
A. Report on daily oil samples from C.C. Wakefield
B. Summary of stops
C. Table showing speed and progress
D. List of records

APPENDIX "D"

Records Established Montlhery July 1-8 1957

Distance	Time	Driver on completion	H.M.S. 1/100	Distance Kms	Kms/H	M.p.h.	Observations
	96 H 4 days	Horrocks		11,572.965	120.55	74.91	Record raised by 12.4%
	120 H 5 days	Threlfall		14475.451	120.63	74.95	Record raised by 13.7%
15000 Km.		Riviere	124.33.58.59		120.42	74.82	Record raised by 13.4%
10000 Miles		Threlfall	133.42.34.71		120.36	74.79	Record raised by 13.2%
	144 H 6 days	Simpson		17341.537	120.36	74.79	Record Raised by 13.3%
20000 Km		Chambers	165.56.23.35		120.53	74.89	New record established
	168 H 7 days	Horrocks		20250.512	120.54	74.90	New record established

The A35 record attempt may have begun as a student stunt but, as this memorandum shows, it was taken very seriously and delivered the results.

BMC Competitions Department Secrets ...

ANNUAL REPORT - COMPETITIONS DEPARTMENT.

1956 - 1957.

During the year 1956/7, the competition world proved to be very disturbed. At the beginning the effects of French "Post Le Mans Jitters" were just finally wearing off when the Suez crisis and petrol rationing were upon us. As this eased, the Portago accident in the Mille Miglia brought fresh dislocation, this time from Italy.

We started off extremely well with the Liege-Rome-Liege, with a 13th and 14th in G.C., Novices prize, second in Coupe des Dames, and second for team prize. This was a 100% M.G. venture.

The Austin A.105 was put into production in August and gave us a very good chance in rallies in the Standard Touring Class.

Bearing in mind the Austin possibilities for the Monte Carlo Rally, a sortie was made with three A.105's and a Magnette in the Viking in September. The Austins were rather large for the event and suffered from core - plug and radiator trouble. Smaller cars would have done better, and it was decided that any further participation in this rally would be with small cars.

The scene was set for the Monte Carlo Rally with a strong team of three A.105's, one Magnette and a Morris Minor 1000 when the Suez crisis hit us. A considerable amount of money had been spent already on the works cars and those of private owners when the event was cancelled.

In order to show the flag during the "no petrol period", we entered the Sestriere Rally with three cars, and assisted three private entries. The event was marred by the Italian organisers' disregard of the rules, and the British cars were outclassed by Grand Touring Cars on the speed circuits. In short, the Rally did little to test the endurance of the cars or the crews.

The R.A.C. Rally was cancelled, but the department kept itself occupied with a surprising variety of B.M.C. cars which needed attention for the coming season. The motoring enthusiast did not lose faith.

The Tulip Rally suffered by reason of the fact that the German authorities cut out many of the timed tests and as a result the cars were not tested for stamina as much as we had hoped. The best we could do were third and fourth in classes G. and H., both in Austins.

We were well prepared for the Alpine, but the event was cancelled due to floods in the Alps which were so extensive as to make re-routing in the time available impossible. The Italian authorities, who had withheld permission to run the event in their territory, reversed their decision at the last moment.

We thus participated in four of the Touring Championship rallies.

A single car was again run in the Lyons Charbonnières and for the second year running collected the Coupe des Dames.

Works-tuned private entries collected many awards in races and rallies, and many of the owners are so satisfied with their vehicles that they have been responsible for purchases of similar cars by friends.

/The

-2-

The department has dealt with many enquiries concerning tuning of B.M.C. cars from all parts of the world. Jobs on private cars handled in the department during the year amounted to 59.

It is felt that we should restrict our entries to the classic rallies :-

    Monte Carlo.
    R.A.C.
    Tulip.
    Alpine.
    Liège-Rome-Liège.

with continued support for private owners in all forms of motoring sport.

We should attempt the hat trick in the Lyons Charbonnières with one car as before.

We have now attracted a team of drivers who are competent in every sort of event, and who place the interest of the Corporation and the car they happen to drive before their personal ambitions. As a result of the "esprit de corps" we can rely on the maximum help for our ladies' crews, and our best placed cars receive the maximum support permissible during the event.

The money spent in U.S.A. has been put to good use. The M.G.A.'s won the team prize at Sebring for the second year running, though we understand there is room for improvement in race control. The Morris Minor 1000 team win in the Canadian Winter Rally showed the potential of the car.

Record-breaking went smoothly, and achieved the desired public recognition with the A.35 at Montlhéry and EX.179 and EX.181 in Utah.

It is to be hoped that the D.O.H.C. B.series engine will not be delayed, as not only are our rivals about to produce more potent models, but many M.G. owners are only keeping their 'A' series until they can obtain a faster car made by the same factory.

The F.I.A. have awarded the title of "Lady Touring Champion 1956" to Mrs. Nancy Mitchell, who drove all the events in that year in an M.G.

A typical example of the annual reports I sent out to members of the Competitions Committee. I wonder if the paragraph about drivers putting the interests of the Corporation and car before personal ambition would apply today?

B.M.C. SUCCESSES IN THE GERMAN RALLY

British Motor Corporation cars took six awards in the German Rally which finished at Baden—Baden over the weekend.

Austin Healey 3000s came first (David Siegle-Morris and Stuart Turner), second (David Morley and B. Hercock) and third (Pat Moss and Ann Wisdom), in the class for Grand Touring cars over 2000 c.c. Pat and Ann had the misfortune to take a wrong turning on a timed section which lost them a number of points and reduced them to third place in their class and the Coupe des Dames.

Peter Riley and Tony Ambrose driving an MGA 1600 scored a notable success against strong competition from nine German entries when they drove the car into second place in the Grand Touring class for 1301 c.c. to 2000 c.c. cars. On the St. Jean circuit hill-climb during which the rain sheeted down turning the road almost into a river, Peter Riley drove magnificently to achieve a time only one second slower than the fastest car in the class.

An Austin Healey Sprite driven by John and Norma Sprinzel came second in the class for Grand Touring cars of 851 to 1300 c.c.

3rd October, 1960

B.M.I.0.

Issued by the Press and Public Relations Offices
THE BRITISH MOTOR CORPORATION LIMITED
Cowley, Oxford and Longbridge, Birmingham
Telephone: Oxford 77777 and Birmingham Priory 2101

A press release issued after the 1960 German Rally; the public relations people usually managed to get Donald Morley's name right.

BMC Competitions Department Secrets ...

                                    Constabulary Headquarters,
                                           Wootton Hall,
                                             Northampton.

LIÈGE - SOFIA - LIÈGE - Team Leaders' Appreciation

1. **DOCUMENTATION**

    The Yugoslavs and the Bulgars are both pretty 'hot' and you must have -
    - (i) <u>Two</u> Transit Visas for Yugoslavia.
    - (ii) <u>One</u> Visa for Bulgaria.

        The Visa stamped in the Passport <u>must</u> show entrance at KALOTINA and exit via GJUESHEVO.
        If this is not so, get it changed at once, or you will be held up at Customs and the time loss may put you out of the rally.
    - (iii) International Driving Licence, (grey book).

2. **HOW THE TIMING WORKS**

    I hope that you have fully appreciated the implications of Article 4(a). If not, try this exercise!

    Take Table II on page 39, and assume your starting time from SPA is 10.42 p.m. (as it may be for some of us). Add the times allowed for the stages cumulatively to 10.42 p.m. which, if you are not late, (and make up the time you will inevitably lose over the MOISTROCCA!), gives you an E.T.A. at ZAGREB of 03.02 a.m. - by which time reference to Table 1 on page 38 will show you that the control has been shut for over 2½ hours, and you've had it!

    In other words, if you do not consistently average a lot more than the set average <u>and</u> continue to build up your time in hand, you will not be penalised for being late on the road, you will just be excluded because the control will be shut when you arrive!

    In addition there is the neat trick of 'neutralisation'.

    Austria is 'neutralised' and that is good, because we can then have enough time to eat. However, Garot proposes to 'neutralise' the fast road between the Vivione and the Gavia, so turning them into timed climbs without letting it so appear in the Regulations.

    These are the neatest stratagems ever devised for 'hoodwinking' the authorities "on paper", yet ensuring that the Liège remains the greatest road-race ever!

    As in France last year, you fix your own time of booking-in, (and simultaneously booking-out), between the times that the controls are shown as being open in your road-books, but with this important difference - holding the schedule only, won't keep you in the rally.

    For instance, on the run to SOFIA, starting at 10.42 p.m. you would have to make up 2 hrs. 32 mins. on schedule to arrive in time to be booked in.

    In fact, we want to aim at making up around 6½ hours.

    <u>Not all drivers have appreciated this point, so don't chat about it outside the team.</u>

A typical page of notes from John Gott – I think his address, top right, helped to get driver attention! The comments on timing are worth studying – basically, the system meant that if you took the full times shown as being allowed between controls (the figures they probably showed to the police), you would arrive at a control to find it had closed some hours earlier! 'Neutralisation' was equally crafty. If, say, there was a twisty section following an easy stretch, the latter would be 'neutralised'; i.e. set at legal limits. This meant there was time to eat ... but it also meant that the twisty section became a flat-out one. One year the organisers announced, almost with tears in their eyes, that the authorities had forced them to introduce secret speed checks. They then silently held up a card with the check locations on it. Is it any wonder that people involved in the Liège go misty-eyed at the mention of the rally?

1955 to 1961: FOUNDATION STONES by Marcus Chambers

Although Pat and Ann had won outright, this publicity leaflet on the Liège win could not resist mentioning every other award won. The left-hand column had a not-so-sly dig at the competition.

LIÈGE—ROME—LIÈGE RALLY 1960   LE MARATHON DE LA ROUTE

Make	Starters	Finishers
Alfa Romeo Giulietta	10	—
Alpine (Renault)	2	—
Austin Seven	1	—
Austin Healey 3000	4	3
Austin Healey Sprite	3	1
Auto Union	3	1
B.M.W.	2	—
Borgward	3	—
Citroën	6	3
Ford	3	—
Jaguar	2	—
Lancia	3	—
Lloyd	1	—
Lotus	1	—
Mercedes	3	—
MGA	2	—
Morris Mini-Minor	1	—
Panhard	3	—
Peugeot	3	—
Porsche	14	3
Renault	2	—
Simca	1	—
Triumph	4	1
Volvo	6	1
	83	13

THE AUSTIN MOTOR COMPANY LTD.
AUSTIN MOTOR EXPORT CORPORATION LTD.
LONGBRIDGE · BIRMINGHAM · ENGLAND

LIÈGE—ROME—LIÈGE RALLY 1960
The British Motor Corporation proudly presents the winner...

Liège-Rome-Liège 1960. Pat Moss and Ann Wisdom take a corner in fine style in their Austin Healey 3000.

B.M.C. Results and Awards:

AUSTIN HEALEY 3000 — outright winner
1st, 5th and 10th in general classification.
1st, 2nd and 3rd, class for 2,500 to 3,000 c.c. cars.
COUPE DES DAMES.
Manufacturers' team prize.
Inter-Ecurie team prize. Ecurie "Safety Fast".

AUSTIN HEALEY SPRITE
3rd in general classification.
1st, class for 851 to 1,000 c.c. cars.

AUSTIN HEALEY
3000—Pat Moss/Ann Wisdom.
      D. Seigle-Morris/V. Elford.
Sprite—J. Sprinzel/J. Patten.
INTERLAND TROPHY FOR GREAT BRITAIN.

The first international event for Pat Moss was the 1955 RAC Rally when she joined BMC after Triumph refused to pay her expenses. Pat is seen here with her MG TF and co-driver Pat Faichney.

BMC Competitions Department Secrets …

Another fine example of the analytical skills of John Gott, this time for an Alpine Rally.

<u>Coupes des Alpes 1961.</u>   Team Leader's Summary

My view is that this rally, like the 1960 one, will be won on the 'Quatre Chemins' Section, i.e. between C.H.12 and C.H.13; (MOST appropriate!) on the last stage.

Recollect - last year 14 cars came up to the section with the chance of a Coupe. Six made the section 'clean', and of those six, four had the advantage of being allowed a minute's lateness, which they will not get this year. Three were only one minute late, two being allowed the extra minute's lateness. The rest - way out.

Of the Healey, Pat and John spun; Pat made it by 9 seconds; John was 25" adrift. Don would have been as good with all four gears.

It seems therefore as though a non-spinning Healey can do the section 'clean'. Make sure you do!

Another very sticky section is Breno to Bagolino, also in the second stage. Also Vivione - very rough.

Obviously therefore both car and crew must be saved for these vital sections. Remember, it's no good doing fantastic times in the tests if neither you nor the car still have the same 'edge' when it comes to the stages which really matter.

The Alpine is a rally which is still won 'on the road' and not in a few kilometres of 'sprinting'. In other words, a 'Head' rather than a 'Boot' rally: better still - a well-chosen mixture of the two!

<u>First Stage</u>

As this is largely new country in parts, I have done the whole of it on my recce.

I don't think that there is anything to worry a competently driven '3000', but there is quite a lot of rough stuff, and 'competently driven' means making up time on the good roads to save the car over the rough by going slow.

Navigation can be tricky in places, so I have tried to produce notes which will take you round without having to follow too closely on the map.

A word about speedo distances.

These can only be a guide, for they are only completely accurate when applied to the same car, using the same speedo as that from which the notes were made. Moreover, if you do not know the exact position of the controls on the recce, your distances can be way out.

Do not therefore rely 100% on my distances quoted, BUT - do not pass by a junction or fork shown in the notes without checking it off, even if the distance doesn't accord with your speedo. We put in the forks etc. because we felt that they were important enough not to be missed and some of them aren't obvious.

On the stages where one can go over the 'top average', I have included a top average time as a guide for you. I have also done this on the bottom average in some sections. If you don't want to rely on these figures completely, you are not obliged to do so, but if you have time in hand over them, you should be O.K.

Distances-
Some of the Club's distances were very shaky. These I have checked with them, and the two worst, Thones to La Clusaz (5km out!) and La Clusaz to Pralong, (Le Reposoir), have been put right I hear this morning. This is the main reason for the delay in getting out the notes.

Finally, don't get muddled with the Liaison and Selectif times. What really matters is the time at the end of the Stages, C.H.2, C.H.3., C.H.9 and C.H.13 up to St. Michel-des-Portes and C.H.8, C.H.16 and C.H.17 afterwards. We almost came unstuck here last year; not again, please. You will note that there is apparently no penalty for early arrival. I have taken this up with the Club, so don't worry about it until we get a 'gen' answer.

Note also that this stage also starts 'easy' and finishes 'tough'!

John Gott

1955 to 1961: FOUNDATION STONES by Marcus Chambers

As another note from John Gott makes clear, tyres were of major concern on the Alpine. Dunlop's David Hiam – who was a huge help to the team and a fine driver himself – said that the Duraband problem put years on him.

From: GOTT   To: CHAMBERS.

Subject: <u>TYRES FOR B.M.C. 'WORKS' HEALEY 3000 TEAM IN ALPINE RALLY, 1961.</u>

1. We cannot afford to ease up in any of the tests.

2. Therefore, assuming a b.h.p. of 200 and judging by last year's lap times, we must cater for each car doing three laps of Monza at between 2' 10" and 2' 15", i.e. around 6½ minutes at a lap speed of between 95 and 100 m.p.h., with around 130 m.p.h. on the straights.

3. We should take the test at around 5 p.m. on June 26th., when it is unlikely to be wet and probably the track will be more than warm with the full heat of the Italian sun on it all day.

4. On arrival at Monza, the cars will have done 1372 km/850 miles from the start and may well be due for a change of tyres anyhow.

5. More important - what tyres should they change to?

6. Last year we used Durabands for Monza, but were averaging laps at around 2' 16", whilst the test was taken in the cool at about 6.30 a.m. and the tyres had only covered 1000 km/650 miles from the start.
Further, maximum speeds were only around 124 m.p.h. on the straights.

7. Even so, both David Hiam and the drivers were happy to get off the track without trouble considering the number of Durabands which had thrown treads in earlier rallies, (Tulip and Acropolis).

8. We can afford no tyre troubles at the speeds we will have to use at Monza, so what is the form?

9. Unless Dunlops have other ideas, the use of a 'braced tread' tyre, i.e. Durabands, for Monza seems inadvisable.
The potential speeds liable to be reached seems to necessitate the use of Racing tyres.

10. These are probably not so good for the rest of the rally, with worse grip on loose surfaces and inferior wearing resistance as compared with Durabands.
However, if it is decided to use Racing tyres, I think one change at Monza should see us through.
The distances involved are,

         Marseille to Monza   1371 km / 850 miles.
         Monza to Cannes   1660 km / 1020 miles.

11. A possible alternative is to use Racing tyres for the Monza test and change back to Durabands after it.
The run from Biella to Monza is 118 km, for which 2h. 21' is allowed. The crews should have at least 30' in hand, possibly more if the Autostrada is used. However, they cannot expect to have as much time in hand as last year, when the run was made in the early morning before too much traffic had got on the roads.
The run from Monza to Schilpario, (which includes much Built-Up area, apart from Bergamo), is 105 km for which 2h. 5' is allowed. The crews should have between 10' - 15' to spare, but it would be safer to work on the lower figure.
During the hour in which the cars are in parc ferme at Monza, the Dunlop boys would have to move from the entrance to the exit of the parc.

12. Racing tyres, of course, should not be used unless they have been 'scuffed'. The drivers could do this themselves at Silverstone, (on the G.P. Circuit and at controlled revs.), which test could also be used as a final check on the cars.

A copy of this memorandum is enclosed as you may wish to send it to Dunlops for their comments.

                                                     John Gott.

28-ii-61.

N O T I C E

ABSOLUTELY OFF LIMITS FOR

>PRESIDENTS
>VICE PRESIDENTS
>CHAIRMEN
>MANAGING DIRECTORS
>DIRECTORS
>SALES MANAGERS
>and
>OTHER V. I. P. s.

also

>DRAGSTERS
>SPORTS CAR ENTHUSIASTS
>CALIFORNIAN HOT RODDERS
>KINGS OF SPEED
>HERO RACING DRIVERS
>RACING MECHANICS
>HOT OCTANE OPERATORS
>LIVING DOLLS
>and
>OTHER TALKATIVE HUMANS

AUTHORISED PERSONNEL INCLUDE FOLLOWING

>CHIEF TIME KEEPER
>MG AND A. H. SPOTTERS
>CHART KEEPERS
>TEAM MANAGERS
>MG AND A. H. GENERAL MANAGER AND DIRECTOR
>B. M. C. TEAM MANAGER

A notice displayed in the pits at Sebring. Despite the bantering tone, the ventures to America were always enjoyable.

1955 to 1961: FOUNDATION STONES by Marcus Chambers

The first event for the new BMC Competitions Department was the 1955 Monte Carlo Rally. Here 'The Three Musketeer' Magnettes were crewed by (left to right): Reg Holt and Willy Cave with third crew member Alan Collinson, Len Shaw and Freddie Finnemore, Geoff Holt with Stan Asbury and John Brooks. The cars were actually prepared by Syd Enever's Development Department next door before the Comps Shop was fully operational.

Standard Group 1 Austin Westminsters took part in the 1955 Monte Carlo Rally prepared at Abingdon. Here, Sam Moore sprints to stop the clock; he and Mort Morris-Goodall finished 232nd – things could only get better.

An MG Magnette on the 1955 Tulip Rally: note the large protective hoods over the two fog lamps and two large externally mounted horns.

1955 to 1961: FOUNDATION STONES by Marcus Chambers

Picking up the pieces, Monte Carlo Rally 1956. Pat Moss with Joan Johns and Doreen Rich after running out of brakes on their Austin Westminster. Pat was in the rear seat on this her first Monte.

Gerry Burgess swings his Austin Westminster round a downhill hairpin on the 1956 Monte Carlo Rally, with Sam Croft-Pearson and Ian Walker. They finished 82nd.

Special goodies fitted to the Austin Westminster of Mike Couper for the 1956 Monte Carlo Rally, including revolving propeller wipers for the lights. The car won the Concours de Comfort.

Knobbly tyres were developed out of the Monte Carlo Rally. Tyresoles produced a special remould with fine wire that became more exposed as the tread wore down in order to improve grip as the cars neared Monte Carlo.

1955 to 1961: FOUNDATION STONES by Marcus Chambers

The MGA team for the 1956 Liège-Rome-Liège; left to right: John Milne/Richard Bensted-Smith, Gerry Burgess/Sam Croft-Pearson, Nancy Mitchell/Anne Hall, John Gott/Chris Tooley. The photo was taken outside the Morris dealer in Liège. Gott was the best placed finisher at 13th overall.

BMC Competitions Department Secrets ...

Grand Prix driver Ken Wharton hurries a works Riley Pathfinder up Prescott during the 1956 RAC Rally.

Jack Sears on Prescott during the 1956 RAC Rally with the Austin A50. Two years later he took an A105 to victory in the first British Saloon Car Championship. Note the additional windscreen wiper above the screen for emergency use in case the standard wipers failed.

1955 to 1961: FOUNDATION STONES by Marcus Chambers

Nancy Mitchell was recruited into the team from HRG in 1956 by Marcus Chambers who encouraged the rivalry with Pat Moss. Nancy brought the team its first Ladies' Prize on the Lyons-Charbonnieres Rally with an MGA.

BMC Competitions Department Secrets ...

Marcus Chambers wanted to build a special edition MG Magnette with a twin cam engine, lightweight panels and knock-off wheels. The nearest he got to it was when he entered Nancy Mitchell on the 1956 Tulip Rally and a scrutineer excluded her after running a magnet over the car and discovering that most of it was made of alloy panels. Nancy is seen here with her favourite Magnette at the Eight Clubs Race Meeting at Silverstone in 1957.

1955 to 1961: FOUNDATION STONES by Marcus Chambers

Nancy Mitchell receives the European Touring Car Ladies' Award for 1956 from John Thornley, MG boss, with John Gott, left, Joan Johns and Marcus Chambers at the annual MG Car Company dinner at London's Grosvenor House.

Total reliability for seven days, despite being driven flat out, resulted in a crop of class Land Speed Records in 1957; this is Cambridge undergraduate (and later Castrol's Rally Manager) Ray Simpson in the very standard Austin A35 prepared at Abingdon.

1955 to 1961: FOUNDATION STONES by Marcus Chambers

The 1957 Liège and Alpine rallies were the first events for the new Austin-Healey 100/6; this is Nancy Mitchell with Anne Hall arriving in 15th place on the Liège. In 1958 Pat Moss finished fourth and won the Ladies' Prize. Ann Wisdom found the big Healey floor so hot that there were sections in Yugoslavia where she sat sideways with her feet hanging out of the window!

Austin A105 wins the 1957 Mobil Economy Run, achieving 33.60mpg. George Kendrick and co-driver Pamela Wright receive their trophy from Mrs Brown (wife of the Mobil boss) with Col Stanley Barnes, the RAC Steward, left. The Economy Run attracted significant publicity in its day and was supported by most manufacturers.

Downhill all the way – a works Riley 1.5 on an icy descent of an Alpine Col on the 1958 Monte Carlo Rally. Winter conditions were so bad that all 10 Abingdon entries failed to finish.

1955 to 1961: FOUNDATION STONES by Marcus Chambers

John Gott hustles his MGA Twin-Cam towards the Cortina control on the 1958 Liège, a road that has changed little and is still used by historic rallies today.

BMC Competitions Department Secrets ...

Night arrival at the end of the 1958 Liège, John Gott and Ray Brookes emerge from their MGA Twin-Cam looking somewhat shattered, but pleased to finish 9th.

1955 to 1961: FOUNDATION STONES by Marcus Chambers

Tommy Wisdom and Douglas Johns tried out the new Sprite on the Monte Carlo Rally of 1959 and finished 63rd. Tommy's daughter Ann, co-driving Pat Moss, finished 10th in an Austin A40.

BMC Competitions Department Secrets ...

With cut finger, this is John Gott and the MGA Twin-Cam coupé on the Monte Carlo Rally in 1959; he skidded off at an icy section and failed to finish.

Can we fix it? Co-driver Stuart Turner beside the smashed hub of John Milne's MGA Twin-Cam on the 1959 Alpine Rally.

1955 to 1961: FOUNDATION STONES by Marcus Chambers

Pat Moss drove so many events in this Morris Minor that she called it 'Granny' – here, it's on the way to 26th place on the 1959 RAC Rally. The previous year Pat had finished 4th and won the Ladies' Prize in the same car.

'Granny' also competed on British club events – Pat Moss and Stuart Turner are here on the 1960 Cats Eyes Rally, which the pair won with 10 minutes to spare the previous year! In 1959 they had also given the new Mini its national rally debut by winning outright the Mini Miglia Rally.

1955 to 1961: FOUNDATION STONES by Marcus Chambers

The Morley brothers on a pioneering run – the start of the Mini era with an 850 Mini Minor heading for 33rd place on the 1960 Monte Carlo Rally. Don Morley recalls: "You would not believe how slow it was at the beginning – the slowest rally car I ever drove. The early cars were pleasant enough to drive, the steering was particularly good, and there was nothing else quite like the agility you got behind the wheel of a Mini – but they were so underpowered. And, of course, the early cars leaked badly, the floors were not sealed properly, and everyone who rallied one would get icy water around their feet. On the race tracks the early Minis broke wheels but frankly we did not have enough power to break the wheels. When you consider that the Mini-Coopers on the 1968 Monte had 90bhp or more at the wheels it was a fantastic transformation."

Pat Moss runs down into Monaco in 1960 with 'Alf', her red Austin A40, in which she finished 17th and won the Ladies' Prize. The previous year, driving the A40 she called 'Zoe', she won the Ladies' Prize and finished 10th after some brilliant timekeeping by Ann Wisdom on the final Mountain Circuit tests.

1955 to 1961: FOUNDATION STONES by Marcus Chambers

Out of Yugoslavia: Pat Moss in the Dolomites with Ann Wisdom leading the 1960 Liège, heading for the BMC team's first international win and first ever international rally win by a female driver.

BMC Competitions Department Secrets ...

Abingdon's tea break on the 1960 RAC Rally – left to right: David Seigle-Morris, John Sprinzel, Ann Wisdom, spectating John Brown, Pat Moss, privateer David Dixon, and Tony Ambrose

Grim winter: walls of snow line the hairpins at the start of the Turini test on the 1961 Monte Carlo Rally, and the final climb for Pat Moss in her one litre Austin A40.

1955 to 1961: FOUNDATION STONES by Marcus Chambers

Peter Riley and Tony Ambrose finished 28th on the 1961 Monte Carlo Rally with this Austin A40.

Dunlop service – Manager Oliver Speight on the 1961 Monte Carlo Rally.

1955 to 1961: FOUNDATION STONES by Marcus Chambers

Pat Moss at a time control on the 1961 RAC Rally: "If I had not stopped to help Erik with a tyre, I could have won!"

Erik Carlsson and Pat Moss stop for a brief chat whilst trying to beat each other at the top of the 1961 RAC Rally leader board.

1955 to 1961: FOUNDATION STONES by Marcus Chambers

The Morley brothers in full cry up the Rest-and-be-Thankful hill climb on the 1961 RAC Rally, but heading for a rare retirement with rear hub failure.

BMC Competitions Department Secrets ...

Derek Astle and Peter Roberts arrive at Scarborough in their works MG Midget on the 1961 RAC Rally, heading for 8th overall and a class win.

Several sections of the RAC Rally took to the forest in 1961. Although British drivers had dominated the event throughout the 1950s, the Scandinavians arrived to revel in conditions like this. This is David Seigle-Morris deep in the middle of Grizedale Forest, heading for 5th overall with the big Healey.

1961-1967

THE MIDDLE YEARS

STUART TURNER

By the time I joined BMC I'd been involved in motorsport for several years, mainly at club level: publishing a club magazine, organising rallies, marshalling and, above all, competing as a rally navigator. In the '50s it was possible to cram in up to 60 rallies a year – all plot and bash (regularity events were shunned by the top crews) which is perhaps why so many navigators seemed to wear thick glasses. Many events were little more than flat out road races: marvellous!

In those days there was less divide than there is today between top events and club rallies – drivers would often get back from an International and do a club rally the following weekend. This interchange helped me because, through getting to know the drivers, I was lucky enough to be asked to co-drive on many major events such as the Monte and Alpine, and, perhaps most memorably, the Liège, which involved a spine-jarring 96 hour drive to a class win with John Sprinzel in a Sprite. Most of the events were in BMC cars so I knew something about the team and the way it operated. It helped, too, that I occasionally navigated for Pat Moss on UK events; in fact, as Marcus Chambers has mentioned earlier in the book, Pat and I won a rally with an 850 Mini very soon after the Mini's announcement. Not everyone was convinced it would be a rally winner but, having sat alongside Pat, I felt it had potential, I just didn't realise how much ...

60 rallies a year ... heady stuff. The problem was I couldn't do that and study to be an accountant at the same time. Fortunately, through writing articles on rallies for the publication, I was offered a job at what was then *Motoring News*. It was a marvellous introduction to journalism because our small staff did almost everything except stand on street corners selling the thing! Two legends of motoring journalism, Bill Boddy and Denis Jenkinson, worked on the sister publication, *Motor Sport*, on the next floor.

It was whilst I was at *MN* (as Sports Editor, no less) that I was lucky enough to sit alongside Erik Carlsson when he won the 1960 RAC Rally in a Saab. He was the only driver to do Britain's very first special stage within the target time, which gave me an inkling of just how quick the Scandinavians were.

Then came my big break. I got a call to visit John Thornley, General Manager at MG. After a brief interview I was invited to become BMC Competitions Manager. I didn't know I was even in the frame for the job. Looking back, maybe a mild reputation for 'rallymanship' helped; not cheating, but pushing the regulations to the limits, although I'm not sure John Thornley was convinced I was the man for the job and think it was really an endorsement by Marcus that clinched it, for which I'll always be grateful.

As an avid enthusiast, going to work at the MG factory at Abingdon where the famous octagon featured everywhere, was like a dream. I was 28, and suddenly found myself working with industry legends, including Alec Hounslow who had been a riding mechanic with Nuvolari. And they were going to pay me £1250 a year to do so. Magic!

BMC Competitions Department Secrets ...

John Thornley was a great person to work for – well-liked, as I saw when he gave me a whistle stop tour of the factory; enthusiastic and energetic, yet with that rare but precious management skill : knowing when to get out of the way. I am sure he had his problems with Longbridge, not least when it was tried to inflict a Mini-based MG sports car on him, but he kept politics well out of my hair.

We had an annual Competitions Committee meeting for which I drafted the agenda. John and I then made sure that people like John Cooper – a huge enthusiast who became a good friend – and to a lesser extent, Donald Healey, were on board and in agreement with what we wanted to do. Thus armed, George Harriman and Alec Issigonis, the two key players on the Committee, didn't really stand a chance and we almost always got what we wanted. After the meetings I wrote the minutes to go out under John's name and was then left to get on with things. That period left me with a firm conviction that flexibility and a lack of bureaucracy is vital if a motorsport programme is to succeed, which usually means keeping it away from mainstream systems.

When I arrived at Ford some years later I found an internal memo saying: "BMC spends whatever is necessary on motorsport". It wasn't quite like that but whilst I don't think we wasted money, finance was never a major issue. It helped that Norman Higgins, the accountant at Abingdon, became a good friend and, in fact, godfather to our first daughter.

By the time I arrived, Marcus had created a great team at Abingdon led by Doug Watts, who I'm quite sure had been asked by John Thornley to keep a fatherly eye on me because I had absolutely zero management experience. Doug could not have done a better job. For all my eagerness to be a new broom, given the way the place functioned there was no need for major change to the operation, although two occurred almost naturally and would have happened even if Marcus had stayed on. The first was that I reduced the range of cars entered on events. In those days there were two objectives: to win a rally, and provide a reason for a success ad for the Monday morning papers. If you hadn't got an outright rally winner then a class win or two, or a team prize could be made to look significant, so the Department had sometimes gone on events with half-a-dozen different makes, all of which had to be supported and serviced, even though the extent of spares carried was nothing like that seen later in world rallying. This policy changed as soon as it became obvious that, in the Mini-Cooper and the Austin-Healey 3000, BMC had cars capable of outright wins.

The second change I made followed almost naturally from the first. Once we had rally winners we didn't need a scatter gun approach to achieve class wins, so required fewer drivers. But for cars capable of winning outright we needed drivers who were able to spend a lot of time recceing. It is perhaps not an exaggeration to say that this requirement resulted in the drivers evolving from 'Gentlemen' into 'Players', similar to what happened in other sports around that time. This is not in any way to denigrate the 'Gentlemen' because they were quick, but, as an example, the Morley brothers – who, with their meticulous planning and organised approach to events would have been the perfect crew for the tough Liège – simply wouldn't do it. Why? Because it clashed with the harvest and, as farmers, they had their priorities right.

My driver changes were hastened when Ford offered Pat Moss and David Seigle-Morris not only more money but the chance to drive the Cortina, which was showing potential. And so what became the key trio of Paddy Hopkirk, Rauno Aaltonen and Timo Makinen was created. The three arrived by different methods. I'd known Paddy for some years from UK rallying, and we'd even been together in the winning team on an RAC Rally in Standard Pennants, so when he wrote saying he wanted to get his hands on an Austin-Healey 3000, I was delighted to sign him up. Actually 'sign up' is perhaps the wrong phrase because I'm proud of the fact that I never signed a formal, legally binding contract with any driver; at most we had an exchange of letters. Naive? Not really, just that you could rely on someone's word and, in any case, I never reckoned there was much point brandishing a contract in an effort to force someone to drive for you if they didn't really want to.

Rauno arrived by a different route. Just before I took over the Department, I sat with Derek Astle in a 3000 on a Polish Rally and we happened to

1961 to 1967: THE MIDDLE YEARS by Stuart Turner

be running next number to Eugen Bohringer in a works Mercedes. As we waited to start one loose stage, I was puzzled to see Eugen swap places with his young co-driver, Rauno Aaltonen. After noting the rapid time he achieved, I came away with Rauno's phone number and found a seat for him on the '62 Monte with Geoff Mabbs in a works-supported Mini-Cooper. Rauno got it up to third place before a clipped corner put them out. I remember that this performance left us somewhat awestruck because we simply hadn't been used to fighting for the lead.

After sitting with Erik Carlsson, and then watching Rauno's efforts, I didn't need Einstein to tell me that maybe something special was happening in Scandinavia. It followed that I didn't reply with a brusque "no" when Raoul Falin, the amiable Morris dealer in Helsinki, popped into my office and asked if I could find a car for the RAC Rally for a young Finn he was helping; someone by the name of Timo Makinen. We found a Mini and, with Aaltonen translating because Timo spoke virtually no English, firmly told him to just potter round and not bend anything. He pottered round ... to seventh overall and a class win. Maybe this was another star in the making...?

In those days (that phrase again; at least I managed to avoid adding 'good' and 'old') entries for the Monte had to be in before the RAC Rally had ended. As a thank you for her amazing race efforts with her own Mini, we'd entered Christabel Carlisle on the '63 Monte in an Austin-Healey. After the RAC I persuaded her to switch from driving what was to have been a Sprite to co-driving this unknown Finn in a 3000. Now, I don't want to upset 3000 owners, but there is a case to be made for not allowing the cars out if a sparrow has peed on the road ... Timo maintains that Christabel told him to go faster – downhill, on snow and ice. Medals have been awarded for less.

Timo's dramatic drive on the event firmly clinched his place in the team. I can perhaps claim to have coined the phrase 'Flying Finns,' but the idea that I was responsible for their breaks is wrong; talent like that was going to make it without any help from me.

Anyway, that's how the three became the core of the team, although, as you will see from documents in this book, the company needed a little persuading that the BRITISH Motor Corporation should use foreign drivers! Innocent days. I've always believed that the way to keep a race or rally driver on his toes is to give him quick team-mates – I'm sure the rivalry helped spur on our drivers, although considering what competitive people they were, it was nice that they remained remarkably friendly. It perhaps helped that I usually paired the foreigners with British co-drivers, partly because I thought they were the best at the time and also because I believed it would help team communication. Timo's limited English at the time sometimes had fringe benefits. He came with me to a Knowldale Car Club dinner and, in my speech, I mentioned that Timo had been learning English specially for the evening. On my cue, he stood up and announced "BMC builds to win", the advertising slogan of the time. It brought the house down.

Although the 3000 continued to produce good results, that period has mainly become linked with the Mini and the Monte Carlo Rally. I'd seen from Rauno's push to third place before crashing what the Mini-Cooper could do, and we went into the '64 Monte reasonably optimistic, albeit worried about a strong team of Ford Falcons which were blisteringly quick. On the event Ljungfeldt's Falcon was fastest by over a minute on the tests but, happily, the handicap system (some events were besotted with them at the time) put Paddy, who had driven superbly, into first place.

The timing could not have been better. The term 'Swinging Sixties' had not yet been coined but it was the era of the Beatles, Carnaby Street and all that jazz, and the Mini fitted perfectly into the scene. Paddy's car was flown back in time for car and crew to appear on *Sunday Night at the London Palladium* which had the highest viewing figures of any TV programme at the time. For me personally, standing in Monaco with Alec Issigonis, who'd flown down especially, watching the baby he'd designed winning an event with a team I was managing, was very special indeed. Actually, Jack Daniels should have been standing with us because without his calm backup to the volatile Alec, the Mini would not have been the success it was. Not that the cake needed any icing, but an extra joy was that after the rally we had a meal at which Fangio was present. Graham Hill was there, too, but Fangio's personality dominated the room even though he spoke no English.

The Monte result was a real team effort involving not just the crews and the people in the workshop but also Bill Price and the rest of the staff. And whilst we were spared today's need to genuflect before sponsors arguing over decal sizes, I don't think we could have won without the help of Castrol and, in particular, Dunlop, with David Hiam, a quick driver in his own right, working flat out on our tyre supplies.

When I got back to Abingdon I found the flags flying and ribbed John Thornley that at last the MG people had recognised the Mini. He told me the flags were flying because the Morley brothers had won the GT category in an MGB …

Timo followed up with a Monte win in '65 with what many students of the sport regard as one of the greatest drives of all time. I know I've been accused of bias towards Timo, sometimes by British drivers who perhaps felt they should have had his drives, but he drove the 3000 beyond its potential on the Monte; he won a Monte (and won it again before being excluded), and then went on to win an RAC Rally hat-trick for me at Ford in Escorts. I rest my case.

Then came the '66 Monte where Timo, Rauno and Paddy took the first three places … and were then thrown out! All three cars and crews were flown back for the Palladium show that time and I believe it was only with some difficulty that an invasion of France was averted. Looking back, although the exclusion was based on a lighting technicality, I think it was really because the Minis were so quick on some stages that the organisers thought we had switched cars. What they didn't realise was – and I hope this doesn't sound immodest, but the hell with it if it does – is that we were perhaps better prepared than our rivals. I'm not sure other teams put out garden thermometers to check if certain sections froze overnight, and I'm not sure other teams were as careful in practising the stages at rally times to best know what conditions would be like, say, in the middle of the night. Nor had they, perhaps, got the same ice note scheme in place. As an example, at the top of the glorious Mont Ventoux stage, Donald Morley – who was driving me round – and I found the corners covered with snow. We waited until the other recce crews had left, checked and found the snow was powdered, swept it off the road using the floor mats from our A110, and put the Minis on racers. Not surprisingly, they were fastest.

For what it's worth, a standard car from the Morris showroom in Monte Carlo proved quicker than the rally cars when tested by a journalist. The publicity ran on and on but, believe me, it wasn't deliberately planned: we weren't that clever. One of the BMC chiefs, Lester Suffield, didn't exactly endear himself to the team with the comment that "They'll calm down when they get back home." To return in 1967 and win the Monte again with Rauno was very sweet.

Drivers – and, to a lesser extent, team managers – get the glory for a win, but in a fine example of Abingdon team spirit, one of the mechanics actually won the event for us. Let me explain. Knowing the conditions on one particular corner of a stage was vital in determining tactics, so I'd asked Robin Vokins, one of the mechanics and someone I thought so highly of that I persuaded him to join me at Ford later, to drive to the corner in his service car and phone me with the conditions. When he got there the gendarmes had closed the stage earlier than expected. I'm sure many people would have phoned to say "Sorry, the road's closed." Not so Robin, who parked and then ran to the corner and back – some three or four kilometres – to the ribald amusement of spectators, and then phoned in the conditions. We won the rally by, I think, 13 seconds, and I would argue that it was won by that run by Robin.

I don't want to give the impression that it was just the Monte that was important, although my wife, Margaret, remembers that every Christmas our dining room table was covered with Monte maps. But details of other rallies from those days have already been well documented so don't need repeating here. And, of course, we were also racing, although I was glad to be able to delegate most of that to Peter Browning, a great race tactician and pit manager.

We used to go to Sebring every year, mainly to fly the MG flag. As we were not going to beat Ferraris or Porches outright, the drivers were selected as a reward for services rendered during the previous year. We

1961 to 1967: THE MIDDLE YEARS by Stuart Turner

used to take whatever was mobile in the workshop to Silverstone in November, together with ten or so drivers who were given just a few laps in each car to prove what they could do.

We also took people like John Cooper, Ken Tyrrell (his enthusiasm for motorsport matched John's), and Don Moore (in my book one of the great engine tuners) along to stand out on the circuit observing. Before the 1964 test, Ken asked if he could bring a youngster along. I can still see John Cooper running up and saying "Sign him, sign him" because the youngster concerned doing some quick times was none other than Jackie Stewart.

I was doing the sort of job that, if advertised as vacant, the Post Office would have had to put on extra vans to cater for the applications they'd have received. Yet I was getting restless. When I took over from Marcus I couldn't understand how anyone would want to give up such a job. but maybe there's something about the sport which runs in five to seven year cycles because I was now beginning to feel the same way. As a result of the Monte coverage I'd got cocky about the media side of things and was therefore a shade put out when I was not even considered when the post of Publicity Director came up (in fact, it went to a good friend, Raymond Baxter). A look into the 'Future Models' file didn't help my mood because it suggested that there were no rally winners in the pipeline.

Then, at a London Motor Show, Walter Hayes (the genius behind most of Ford's motorsport success) grabbed me and took me over to meet the Chairman of Ford of Britain, saying "This is the man who gives us all the trouble with the Minis." An offer to go and run the Ford team soon followed. I said "no" mainly because it didn't seem right to switch straight to our main rival. Such innocence.

I joined Castrol instead where I spent the first six months not working but at Dorland Advertising, undergoing a crash course in advertising – an amazing, slightly-elderly youth training scheme that was invaluable experience but which I'm sure wouldn't operate today. I kept some links with BMC because I took Castrol into a motor club support programme that continued the forums with the drivers we'd been running for some years. At one of these, a man came up and said I should give his son a drive because he was quick. I made the usual 'don't call us, we'll call you' comments – and didn't find out until I got to Ford that it had, in fact, been Roger Clark's father.

I remained happily settled at Castrol until being part of the organising committee of the London to Sydney Marathon, and then marshalling on it in Turkey, Afghanistan, India and Australia, rekindled my enthusiasm for the sport. When Walter Hayes made another offer, I accepted.

I realised that motorsport life at Ford was going to be different from that at BMC when the first member of staff to greet me said "Welcome. I am your Financial Controller". At that point, I didn't even know what such a person did.

I called my autobiography *Twice Lucky* because, without fully appreciating it at the time, I joined Ford just as the Escort was coming on song. But I will never forget the joys of the years spent working at Abingdon with a marvellous back-up team and such fine drivers and cars.

Visit Veloce on the web – www.veloce.co.uk
Details of all our books • Newsletter • New book news • Special offers

TELEPHONE:
ABINGDON
251 P.B.X.

THE MG CAR COMPANY LTD
ABINGDON WORKS
ABINGDON-ON-THAMES
PROPRIETORS: MORRIS MOTORS LTD

TELEGRAMS:
EMGEE
ABINGDON

YOUR REF

OUR REF JWT/GEVC.
24th July 1961.

Stuart Turner, Esq.,
1a Exmouth Road,
Bromley, Kent.

Dear Mr. Turner,

    This is to confirm the arrangements tentatively made on the occasion of your recent visit.

    I would like you to join us as soon after 1st September as you conveniently can to run parallel with Marcus Chambers until his departure at the end of that month. You will then take over the duties of B.M.C. Competitions Manager.

    Your salary for the commencement of your employment will be £1,250 per annum.

    If you will, in your turn, let me know that these conditions are acceptable, we shall then make the appointment public, and it would not surprise me in the least if Ann Clayton was after you for some biographic details!

Yours sincerely,

J W Thornley

My letter of engagement was typical of John Thornley – friendly but direct and to the point. Ann Clayton was handling motorsport PR at the time.

PADDY HOPKIRK LIMITED

MOTOR ACCESSORIES

12 ALFRED STREET
BELFAST 2
N. IRELAND

Telephones: 27616 (2 lines)
Telegrams: "Handbrake" Belfast

YOUR REF.:
OUR REF.: PH/AC

5th June, 1962.

Mr. Stuart Turner,
M.G. Car Company,
c/o Hotel Rose The,
La Ciota,
Nr. Marseilles,
Cote D'Azur,
France.

Dear Stuart,

    Rootes demanded all cars be returned to the factory for examination - hence no Sunbeam for the 'Alpine'. I asked Norman if I could drive the Healey, and he said most definitely not.

    I am extremely disappointed to miss the event, and as my contract comes up for renewal with Rootes in August this year, I would be very pleased to hear from you before I make any arrangements for 1962/63. I am very reluctant to leave Rootes from the point of view of my relationship with the Rootes Distributor in Belfast, but Stuart I do want to drive cars which are capable of winning Rallies outright - even if I'm not!

    I can have all the free time I desire for the coming season, and would be very keen on competing for the European Championship. Please contact me when you get back if you are interested.

    Thanks again for the offer.

    Kindest regards,

    Yours sincerely,

P.S. Best of luck in the Alpine

Paddy Hopkirk.

SOLE CONCESSIONAIRES

| BARDAHL | SPEEDWELL | DECOSOL | TIP-TOP | ELVA | DONALD HEALEY | HALDA |
| OIL ADDITIVE | SPEED EQUIPMENT | PRODUCTS | VULCANISING PRODUCTS | CARS | SPEED EQUIPMENT | SPEED PILOT |

When Paddy wrote this letter to me care of the hotel we always used for the Alpine, he was anxious to get behind the wheel of a 3000. I don't think either of us realised just how closely linked to the Mini his name would become.

BMC Competitions Department Secrets ...

Notes for Works Drivers

1. It is your responsibility to have up-to-date passports, competition licences, driving licences and any necessary visas. These must be obtained by you direct NOT through Competitions.

2. Any changes to travel arrangements must be made through Competitions with the sole exception of returns from rallies on which you have broken down, in which case it may be more convenient to work direct with our travel agents. Note that phone calls to them must not be reversed.

3. You will be insured at all times while rallying or recceing for us and a copy of the insurance schedule will be sent to you on request. You are covered for £150 of baggage excluding watches, jewellery, cameras, money and any single article over £50.

4. Maps are regarded as expendable items and are therefore chargeable. However do not have invoices sent direct to us but claim for them on your periodic expense sheets (note that we now have an enormous quantity of 1" maps from previous RAC rallies which can be drawn on before incurring further expense, they are not revised all that often).

5. It is up to the co-driver to provide his own map boards, Eolites, etc. and as these are the normal tools of the trade they are not chargeable.

6. Co-drivers are responsible for the safekeeping of intercom sets and also clocks (this particularly applies when a car has broken down).

7. Whenever you break down and leave a car make sure that the documents (e.g. Green Card and 29C) are left in the roof pocket, which from now on will be a standard fitting.

8. It is the co-driver's responsibility to make sure that report forms are filled in and these must be sent to Competitions within 48 hours of your return to this country, together with a "reminder sheet" for next year. In future these documents will be sent to you before each rally.

9. Co-drivers are responsible for obtaining the necessary trade lists of service points, oil and fuel supplies, etc. although these are often distributed via Competitions.

10. Drivers must not rely on Competitions for a copy of the Regulations for an event, quite often we only receive one or two copies and you should therefore make sure that you are on the mailing list of the Competitions Department of the R.A.C. who usually get bulk supplies and/or on the direct mailing list (to your home address) of Organising Clubs.

11. To maintain continuity, you should only work through the supervisory staff in the Department: in future for overseas drivers (and their co-drivers) work through D. Green, for UK drivers through T. Wellman.

This was issued to all team members soon after I'd taken over from Marcus. Item 8 was an attempt to ensure we didn't forget key points when doing an event the next time. I don't recall item 11 being followed very closely.

- 2 -

12. Remember that servicing a rally is often an onerous job so do not bully mechanics however pressed you may be. You will find that politeness will bring you better results. It is always your responsibility to tell them how long you can spare at a service point.

13. Where crews are sent on reconnaissance runs for the whole team, co-drivers are responsible for providing legible navigation and/or pace notes.

14. Daily and petrol expenses whenever possible will be paid before a rally or recce and adjustments will in future be made afterwards. To avoid unnecessary accounting, adjustments will be made on the cheque for the next rally. Where an outright win entails going on trips to Motor Shows etc. you will be paid at the same daily rate as on a rally, but not for talks to Motor Clubs etc. in this country (although in these cases hotel bills will be met if an overnight stop is necessary).

15. Ten per cent of all prize monies and bonuses is to be paid to the Mechanics' Fund.

16. Work will not be possible on your private cars except in very rare instances, and then only with the authority of the Competition Manager.

17. While every care will be taken with items left in cars, we cannot be responsible for clothes, blankets, pillows etc. which will be thrown out if not claimed within two months. It would help if all your equipment has your name on it somewhere.

18. A competition tie is available which is given to anyone with four works drives in an Abingdon car. If ties get worn they will be replaced provided the old one is handed in.

19. Remember that one of the main reasons for our activities is publicity, so do all you can to maintain good relations with the press. Naturally if you break down there is no need to over elaborate on the reasons, but do not lie to the press.

20. When a driver intends to take his wife on a rally we will be happy to book accommodation provided we are notified early enough for it not to entail extra correspondence. Normally this means four to six months notice because we book Alpine accommodation in February and Monte accommodation in August.

Point 13 followed an incident where "ML and how" in pace notes, to indicate that it was quite a difficult medium left bend, was misread by another crew. They went off while still looking for "and house". Point 20 was the start of my campaign – unpopular in some quarters – not to take wives on rallies. "Sex before an event? Not if it means keeping the scrutineer waiting" was, I think, the joke at the time.

1961 to 1967: THE MIDDLE YEARS by Stuart Turner

BRITISH MOTOR CORPORATION LTD.

MINUTES OF THE NINETEENTH MEETING OF THE COMPETITIONS COMMITTEE HELD AT LONGBRIDGE ON WEDNESDAY, 22ND AUGUST, 1962.

Present:
- Mr. J.W. Thornley. — Chairman.
- Mr. R.A. Bishop.) Members of
- Mr. A. Issigonis.) Committee.
- Mr. S. Turner.)
- Mr. John Gott. — Hon. Member.
- Mr. Donald Healey.) Co-opted.
- Mr. John Cooper.)

Mr. Harriman attended the Meeting for part of the time.

1. **Minutes of last meeting.**

   The minutes of the last meeting were taken as read.

2. **Report on 1961/62.**

   Mr. Turner summarised the achievements and principal events of 1961/2, and Mr. Bishop tabled the summary of B.M.C. Competition achievements through the year, which had been compiled by his Competitions Press Officer.

   Mr. Gott proposed that an appreciation of Mr. Turner's efforts be recorded in achieving in his first year the near impossible by improving on Marcus Chambers' record in his last year.

3. **Budget.**

   It was decided to defer consideration of the budget, largely because this would be dependent upon recommendations made and decisions reached regarding the programme for the ensuing year.

4. **Programme.**

   The policy of concentration on a small number of main events would be continued, and entries would be made in the Liege, the R.A.C., the Monte and the Alpine. Among these events it was to be noted that the Liege continued as the toughest rally, the Monte the most publicised, the Alpine was declining in importance, whereas the R.A.C. was rising.

   In addition to the above, it was agreed that three Morris 1100's should be entered in the Safari, provided that the political climate did not further deteriorate.

   Note was also taken of the rising importance of the Tour de France, a rally which consisted of road sections linking the numerous speed circuits. This was clearly a rally suited to a crew consisting of one rally driver and one circuit driver, and it was decided that B.M.C.'s entry in the forthcoming year should be a co-operative effort between Mr. John Cooper and the Competitions Department.

   Mr. Turner outlined the attempt which had been made to secure the services of Eric Carlsson, and which had finally failed. In his stead we had secured Rauno Aaltonen, who was confidently expected soon to surpass Carlsson in driving ability.

   Messrs. Paddy Hopkirk and Jack Scott had now come over to B.M.C. from Rootes, and, with the departure of Ann Riley, Mrs.

   /Pauline

The first of what became key documents for me. John Thornley and I drew up an agenda and then lobbied people like John Cooper before the meetings, which usually lasted a couple of hours. John Gott had stood down as Team Captain by this time but was still an Hon Member of the Committee. We never clashed but I think he sensed I wanted total control. My lasting memory of John is returning from an Alpine each nervously driving one of the 3000s. We were stopped by a gendarme. I wonder if Chief Constables perhaps have special notes in their passport because the Frenchman said "200kph? That's for airplanes not cars. Allez" – and waved us on.

Point 2 R A (Reg) Bishop was head of publicity so, at this stage, both marketing and engineering – via Alec Issigonis – had input to our activities. Quite properly, too.

Point 4 We'd swallowed the publicity about Hydrolastic suspension and tried very hard to make 1100s into rally cars – Rauno Aaltonen in particular did miles of testing over rough tracks in Wales near Rhayader. A lost cause. We were always glad to co-operate with John Cooper – as suggested here on the Tour de France – because of his infectious enthusiasm. He never flagged and he always had Ken Tyrrell on the sidelines urging him to press for more power. I tried quite hard to get Erik to drive for us, although – having experienced the glorious atmosphere in the Saab team when doing the RAC and then the Canadian Rally with Erik – I sensed somehow that he would stay with Saab. He did, and it was the right decision.

-2-

Pauline Mayman had been brought in as co-driver to Pat Moss, a partnership which was proving to be extremely successful, both in achievement and in the maintenance of harmony within the team.

5. Sebring.

In the 12-hour race the Healey 3000 is capable of finishing high up in General Classification, and the MGB. should win its class. It was decided therefore to prepare three of each of these cars, and to enter two of each in the 12-hour Race. In addition, Mr. Donald Healey would run one Sprite at 1100 cc. in its class. One of the MGB's would be driven by Miss Pat Moss and Mrs. Pauline Mayman; the other by Flaherty and Parkinson. British drivers would be used for all the Healeys, subject to the possible exception of Mr. McQueen. In the 3-hour Race one Sprite and one M.G. Midget would be entered, these being the lightweight standard-looking cars, which ran both as Sprites last year.

At this point Mr. Harriman joined the Meeting.

6. Tuning privately owned cars.

It was agreed that we should continue to divert these requests to Downton, Don Moore, etc., though it was realised that the combined capacity of these sources was insufficient to meet the demand.

It was agreed that U.S. Distributors, one on the West Coast (Qvale ?) and one on the East Coast, should be encouraged to establish tuning centres, and consideration should be given to the establishment in U.S. of a payment-by-results bonus scheme, similar to that operated by the Competitions Department here. Mr. Harriman requested that he should be furnished with notes on the suggested set-up in U.S.

7. Saloon Car Racing.

This was discussed in many aspects, and it was agreed that we should continue to concentrate on the use of the Mini, and not enter the Lists with larger cars. It is consistent with our competition policy that success with the Minis should reflect upon B.M.C. as a whole, and that the best possible publicity was to be derived from the contests between David and Goliath.

8. Service Van.

A scheme for a modestly-sized mobile workshop was outlined, and Mr. Harriman authorised that this should be proceeded with, commenting that he was surprised we had not had one long ago.

9. Pat Moss.

It was agreed that Mr. Turner be authorised to negotiate on the basis of a maximum retainer of £1,500, and should again endeavour to obtain agreement to the exclusive use of B.M.C. products.

10. Rally Championships.

Outright rally wins were to continue to be the main aim. If as the season progressed the World, European, or Ladies Championship appeared to be within our grasp, isolated entries in additional rallies could be considered against the background of the climate prevailing at the time.

/11.

Point 5 Yes, it is the McQueen. He was quick and fitted in well, perhaps because as most of us were too busy to go to the cinema, we didn't really know how famous Steve was so treated him as just one of the team. The Mr Harriman noted as joining the meeting was George Harriman the Chairman.

Point 6 America was obviously a key market for MG and Austin-Healey. Bonus Schemes as suggested were very popular at that time.

Point 7 The Committee was right about the benefits derived from David and Goliath battles on the track with the Mini. Paddy, for instance, electrified the Tour de France mixing it with bigger cars.

Point 8 Just one example of the supportive attitude at the top.

Point 10 A carefully crafted minute that left me with a great deal of freedom.

1961 to 1967: THE MIDDLE YEARS by Stuart Turner

-3-

11. Rally drivers as test drivers.

This matter was to be the subject of separate discussion between Mr. Turner and Mr. Issigonis. It was desirable as a first step that a senior member of the Engineering Department (e.g. Mr. Griffin) should accompany a reconnaissance party, and might subsequently compete, with a view to getting firsthand knowledge of rally conditions and their effects on the vehicles.

12. Rally teams owning non-B.M.C. cars.

Mr. Harriman agreed that regular members of the B.M.C. team should be offered one B.M.C. car per year at staff terms, on condition that they used this vehicle for their personal transport.

13. Any other business.

Mr. Donald Healey referred to an earlier conversation with Mr. Harriman, and it was confirmed that it had been agreed that limited support should be given for private entries at Le Mans, so that if a car were privately entered it could be prepared by the factory and the pit manned by Competitions staff.

Circulation :

Mr. G.W. Harriman.   Mr. W.V. Appleby. (4)
Mr. J.R. Woodcock.   Mr. G.B. Ashton.
Mr. T.A. Sangster.   Mr. A.S. Enever.
Mr. J.F. Bramley.   Mr. J.R. Thompson.
                           Miss Ann Clayton.

                           Mr. J.W. Malone.
                           Mr. M.J. Trodd.
                           Mr. E.M. Gibbs.
                           Mr. J.W. Bache.
All present.   Mr. C. Griffin.

Point 11 Having seen the closeness between motorsport and mainstream at Saab, I tried to encourage this at BMC but with only limited success because mainstream people had more important things to do. I had an ulterior motive – I thought such a liaison would enhance my budget prospects.

Point 12 The wide circulation of the minutes is an indication of the interest in our activities. It was advantageous if other departments we were seeking help from saw that Harriman and Issigonis in particular were on board.

This somewhat brutal note to John Thornley is probably self-explanatory. It was written to brief John prior to a Competitions Committee the next month. Note that problems still existed with a British company associating with French products.

To: ST/DMK   From:
Mr. J.W. Thornley   10.9.63   Mr. Turner

Competition Programme 1964

1. The Opposition

   <u>Triumphs</u> treat International rallies rather like British Club events and are not serious opposition, although the TR4 is a much improved rally machine.

   <u>Sunbeams</u>. The Rapier is getting old for current rallying, as are some of its drivers. It remains to be seen whether the rumoured "Brabham - Imp" materialises as a serious challenge to the Minis.

   <u>Rovers</u> are quietly getting results and their new 2000 saloon could make them more serious opposition although at the moment they haven't got drivers capable of outright wins, unless they use Graham Hill through their B.R.M. link.

   <u>Reliants</u>. Although they won the Austin Healey class on the Alpine, they motor very, very slowly, and their activities are likely to dissolve into a cloud of fibre-glass dust at any moment.

   <u>Volvos</u> have a very strong team. Bohringer in a <u>Mercedes</u> is always a threat and despite rumours that he will be joining Fords, <u>Saabs</u> seem confident that they will still have the redoubtable Carlsson next year.

   Which leaves us with <u>Fords</u>.

   From being a shambles on the Monte Carlo Rally, they have now become a very serious threat indeed, and only Aaltonen's skill prevented them taking a 1, 2 on the Alpine. The Cortina is a good rally tool with the right power to weight ratio, size and ground clearance. Henry Taylor was well placed on the Liege using the Lotus engine and I have a feeling that the 1964 version of the Lotus Cortina will be very serious opposition

   Their connections with Total are proving a psychological advantage because Total garages en route welcome Ford drivers with open arms and lavish supplies of refreshments. (I wonder if we ought to reconsider our attitude over signing with a French company?)

2. Drivers

   In Aaltonen, Hopkirk and Morley we have three drivers unequalled by any other team. Logan Morrison has not matured as I had hoped and next year

BMC Competitions Department Secrets ...

- 2 -

I would like to revert him to a semi-private owner basis getting a fixed payment from us per rally but doing them in his own car.

Timo Makinen, who was brought in as a partner for Christabel on the Monte shows fine form and on the Alpine was equalling Donald's times despite the fact that he had not done a recce and was still finding his feet on tarmac. His drive on the Monte was a classic (as was his T.V. win at Brands Hatch).

As far as the Coupes des Dames are concerned, I feel we must face the fact that Pauline and Val, competent though they are, just don't seem to attract publicity. Pauline drove intelligently on the Alpine but has not improved to the extent that in a Mini Cooper she is ever likely to beat Pat or Ann Hall in Cortinas unless they break down. (I

I feel that a team consisting of Aaltonen, Hopkirk, Makinen and Morley could produce enough high placings for us not to need Coupe des Dame wins to advertise and as at the moment other teams less favourably placed for drivers would be glad to have their services I suggest we drop them after the R.A.C., giving them as much warning as possible.

Pat has got less publicity this year than ever before and if ever she drops out of rallying, perhaps to start a family, then I feel there might be a long overdue drop in interest in the Coupe des Dames. One other angle we might consider is to get Christabel to do two or three of the better known rallies next year.

Events
I would suggest a programme along these lines:

Monte - 4 cars, Tulip - 2, Acropolis - 2, Alpine - 4, German - 2, Polish - 2, Liege - 3 (4 if the Morleys can be persuaded to do it!) Tour de France - 4, Geneva - 2, R.A.C. - 4.

The following points seem relevant:

a) This programme would spread our publicity as widely as possible and would keep our drivers in practice. It is similar to the programme Pat did last year.

b) The co-drivers should be encouraged to write for the Motor, "Autocar", etc., so that the slightly obscurer events (such as the Polish) get adequate coverage (Tony Ambrose already has some contacts along these lines).

c) If it is necessary under S.M.M.T. rules for a trophy to be presented on a rally before we can advertise "Best British Car" then we should ensure that someone donates a cup for any event which at present lacks one.

We didn't realize it at the time but I suppose a drop of interest in Coup des Dames was inevitable once Pat began to demonstrate that really quick women don't need the 'protection' of special awards. As the note re: the Morleys and the Liège indicates, I kept trying – without success – to get them to skip the harvest and do the rally. Their methodical approach would have been perfect for the event.
Point 3c I don't know if buying trophies to win yourself is quite the done thing, but it seemed like a publicity opportunity at a time when we were still happy to cram anything into success ads.

- 3 -

d) The programme would call for fewer total cars entered than this year but by concentrating on top drivers the results could be even better. Saabs with their singleton Carlsson entry have proved that quality not quantity counts. If we rigorously fend off press entries etc. on the Monte (even the clergyman routine is showing diminishing publicity returns) and spend the money on giving our aces longer practice periods, then an outright win instead of 3rd and 6th is not out of reach.

e) It seems high time that our competition adverts told a story and perhaps had a picture instead of reading like a list of Premium Bond winners. For the purely sporting press I think we could take a leaf out of BP's book and use semi-feature ads (their one on Bohringer was superb).

f) The rallies would be spread among the drivers (the Morleys would probably do less than the others because of their farming) but I would suggest that we always use British co-drivers with the Finns and try to work it that, for instance, Hopkirk and Makinen take two cars on one event, Morley and Aaltonen two on the next and so on.

At the moment Scandinavia is undoubtedly producing more top drivers than any other country, but motor sport has become so International that I do not think a couple of Finns in the team is anything to worry about (Mercedes have used Rauno, Triumphs use a Swiss, Ferrari use English drivers and so on). In any case Rauno's father has an Austin agency and Timo is a Morris and Wolseley salesman.

g) If we do not offer our drivers sufficiently active programmes there is always the danger that we might lose them.

h) I hope the Competitions Committee will sanction the roller brake so that we can provide our top drivers with top notch cars.

i) More local publicity ought to be made of our rallying. I know there is the language problem but I am sure that more overseas distributors (if they had enough warning) could throw brief "meet the press" sessions for the team.

I have written at rather long length about next year but the opposition is getting so hot that unless we stay really on our toes we may lose our place at the top of British rallying.

Point d Despite my offhand comment, having two clergymen in a Mini generated useful publicity. A black car with a white roof seemed in good taste at the time.
Point e For some time Competitions didn't feel that BMC's advertising or press relations really did justice to our efforts. We should probably have been told to go away and concentrate on the events.
Point f Again, justifying not being 100 per cent 'British'.

1961 to 1967: THE MIDDLE YEARS by Stuart Turner

B.M.C. COMPETITION COMMITTEE MEETING, 16.10.63.
NOTES ON AGENDA, ITEM 6.

1. Ford competition is emerging at all levels. In Saloon Car racing, the 7-litre Galaxie is unbeatable in the dry, and the Falcon would have won the Monte Carlo if it had started from Paris. The Cortina is a good rally tool with the right power-to-weight ratio, size, and ground clearance. The 1964 version of the Lotus Cortina will be very serious opposition. And the Anglia, in Group 3 tune (where this is permitted, e.g. circuit racing and the Liege) is formidable.

Ford's ground organization, from being a shambles at the time of the '63 Monte, has improved, and is still improving, though they seem, at this moment, to have mishandled their driver situation.

2. The Mini Cooper S. is still capable of giving a good account of itself (c/f Tour de France) and could still win the next Monte. In circuit racing, however, it can no longer "mix it with the big stuff".

ADO.16 and A.40 are outclassed on power-to-weight, as are also ADO.38 and ADO.17.

Even the Austin-Healey 3000 in its current Rally trim with 200 b.h.p. is not theoretically capable of winning International events. That it has done so is a tribute to superlative driving and ground organisation versus a combination of bad luck and clottishness from the opposition (Ferrari/Porsche/Mercedes).

The remaining sports cars are less favourably placed in terms of power-to-weight.

3. To provide an answer to this, three possibilities present themselves:

  (a) An A.40 fitted with an MGB. power unit at 140 b.h.p.
  (b) ADO.41/47 similarly equipped.
  (c) ADO.51/52 with 2.5 litre power unit at 180 b.h.p.

(a) would appear to be the only opportunity to fight Ford on its own ground, but the questions then arise :-

  (i) Is it sense to make a frontal attack ?
  (ii) Would not such a vehicle savour too much of a "stunt" ? It could scarcely be regarded as progressive.

(b) has the merits :-

  (i) That it could be brought into being comparatively quickly.
  (ii) Abingdon already has experience of a similar car, but with 1622 cc. B. series power unit.
  (iii) The sports car public has been wondering for some time (i.e. since Riley One-point-Five successes) why we don't do something of the kind.

(c) is the logical development, but will take some time to achieve. Design is already well advanced, i.e. ADO.51/52, and the power unit could be based on ADO.61, de-stroked.

(Note 1. Cars under (b) and (c) above would run under Grand Touring category and only 100 off would be necessary for homologation. Car (a) would be a Touring car, and production of 1000 would be necessary.)

(Note 2. G.T. class is split, in Monte, Alpine, Tulip and R.A.C., at 1000 cc. and 2500 cc. At Le Mans and Sebring, splits are at 1600, 2000 and 2500. Only in Liege and Tour de France are splits at 1000 and 2000. 2½ litres, therefore, is our best bet under current regulations.)

Point 2 ADO 16 = 1100/1300s. ADO 38 = Face-lifted. Farina models – Austin A55, Morris Oxford, etc. ADO 17 = Austin/Morris 1800s.

Point 3(b) ADO 41/47 were Mk11 Sprites and Midgets. 3(c) ADO 51 was an Austin-Healey version of the MGC which Donald Healey got cancelled. 3(c) ADO 52 was the MGC. The Austin-Healey 3000 drivers were not enthusiastic ...

Point 6 on the agenda refers to the Ford challenge.

BMC Competitions Department Secrets ...

Point 4 John Thornley was not the only one concerned about the lacklustre performance of some models in the BMC range.

-2-

4. It must not be concluded from paras. 1 and 2 above that all is considered lost for 1964. With our present drivers, given only average good fortune, and provided we are selective in the events which we enter, the Cooper S., the Healey 3000 and the MGB., can still carry us through with some success. But to be assured of future and continued ascendancy, cars of better power-to-weight ratio must be provided.

We make no excuse for continually reverting to this theme. The fact must be faced that, in Europe particularly, B.M.C. has an image of being deficient in engine power. The standard (850) Mini lags behind the SAAB; the ADO.38 range is inferior to Peugeot and Volvo; the acceleration of the ADO.16 is not setting the world on fire; and, from all accounts, ADO.17 is not expected to be any better - in this one respect.

5. Any of the cars mentioned in para. 3 above would be capable of :

   (a) Winning International Rallies outright.
   (b) Making a good showing in such events as Sebring and Le Mans.
   (c) Doing well in circuit racing in this country with a "giant killing" act against the privately entered E. types and G.T.O.s.
   (d) Providing the U.S.A. with just what is needed for circuit racing there.

6. All in all, we feel that the 2½ litre MGB. is at once the most logical and forward-looking solution, likely to achieve the most success and have the greatest impact world-wide.

JWT/GEVC.
15.10.63.

1961 to 1967: THE MIDDLE YEARS by Stuart Turner

B.M.C. COMPETITIONS DEPARTMENT.

MINUTES OF MEETING HELD AT EARLS COURT ON 16TH OCTOBER 1963.

Present:
- Mr. G.W. Harriman.   Chairman.
- Mr. A. Issigonis.
- Mr. Brian Turner.
- Mr. J.W. Thornley.
- Mr. A.S. Enever.
- Mr. C. Griffin.
- Mr. John Cooper.

1. Report on 1963.

Lists of successes in the fields both of International Rallies and Saloon Car Racing were circulated. A fair comment is that they made monotonous reading !

2. Programme for 1964.

(a) Racing.

(i) Sebring. It was decided that two MGB.s should be entered in the 12-hour race to run for class win, and that Mr. Donald Healey should run one Gp.III or prototype Sprite in the 12-hour race for the Index of Performance. No entries would be made in the 3-hour race.

If last year's race for Saloon Cars (2 hours on the Friday) is repeated, two Cooper S. would run, to be driven by P. Hopkirk and J. Whitmore. This, apart from other considerations, would assist Mr. Cooper to retain the services of Sir John.

The suggestion that the B.M.C. operation at Sebring should be run by Kjell Qvale was discussed. Final decision was left pending receipt by the Chairman of estimate of cost and also until after he had discussed the matter with Mr. Suffield.

If Qvale were to run Sebring for us, Mr. John Cooper would go to watch our interests.

If the Saloon car race is on, one of the MGB.s would be driven by Hopkirk/Whitmore, the other by Americans.

(ii) Le Mans. One MGB. would run for Class Win and best possible overall placing. One Sprite, to be prepared by Healey, would run for Index.

(iii) Targa Florio. An entry for this would be considered later, to be managed by Mr. John Cooper's stable.

(iv) Saloon Car Racing. This year's programme for the British Saloon Car Championship would be repeated.

Mr. Cooper stated that this year the European Touring Car Championship would be run under F.I.A. auspices, and asked if we should compete for this. This, which would have 1000 cc. and 1300 cc. classes, would embrace five or six races of 6 hours duration. Decision was deferred pending submission of estimate of cost by Mr. Cooper to Mr. Harriman.

Mr. Cooper requested that, to ensure success in these events, the Cooper S. should be produced and homologated with three engine sizes, viz: 1000 cc. with short-stroke crank, 1100 cc. with standard crank and 1300 cc. with long-stroke crank. Mid-January was the next homologation date. This was agreed.

(b) Rallies.

Mr. Stuart Turner's submission for fewer cars in more events, so as to spread publicity and reduce time gaps between successes, was approved. The suggested programme is :

/Monte

Point 2a The Mr Suffield was Lester Suffield who was running BMC operations in North America. It was said that he had had tinted mirrors put in the cloakrooms to make people look healthier and therefore more energetic. They just made me feel jaundiced.

-2-

Monte, 4 cars; Tulip, 2; Acropolis, 2; Alpine, 4; Polish, 2; German, 2; Liege, 4; Tour de France, 4; Geneva, 2; R.A.C., 4. This to be flexible and subject to modification to fit the circumstances as they develop.

A letter was read from B.M.C., Geneva, requesting interest in competition in Austria. Agreed that, following a success in the above programme, one car should be entered in the next succeeding suitable International event in Austria.

3. Drivers.

Hopkirk/Liddon were with us, by agreement, at least until August 1964. Also through 1964 we had the Morley Twins, Aaltonen/Ambrose and Makinen. Undoubtedly, B.M.C. had the best teams in the business.

Some of our drivers, notably Hopkirk, were being tempted by offers from Ford. While, in the circumstances, bids for our drivers were to be expected, the Chairman undertook to discuss the matter with Sir Patrick Hennessey and Mr. Alan Barke, and try to secure that these approaches should be on ethical and businesslike lines.

Mr. S. Turner asked for guidance regarding our women drivers in that Mrs. Mayman, though she had had some success, had not, and would not, reach the Pat Moss level. Furthermore, the importance of Coupes des Dames seemed to be waning. It was agreed that, largely in recognition of past loyalties, Mrs. Mayman and Miss Domleo should be retained for a further year.

4. Revision of Bonus Scheme.

More and more events were securing International status, many of them yet of small importance publicity-wise. Cost of bonus payments had been increasing sharply. A revised scheme was submitted, reducing payments on minor events. This was approved, subject to future review if it should be possible to improve publicity coverage. The revised bonus scale is attached to these minutes.

In those instances where events were split into two or more main categories, e.g. Touring and Grand Touring, the scale would be applied to both categories. This to be subject to revision in the light of experience.

5. Publicity tie-up.

The Tour de France had shown what was possible in terms of local advertising and free-space coverage. Dis-satisfaction had been expressed in certain quarters regarding the feed of news arising from our Competition activities. What was felt to be needed was a full-time Press representative who could participate in the ground organisation of Rallies and Racing, preferably French-speaking, who could use a camera or be accompanied by a photographer, and feed a constant stream of news and pictures to the points most likely to make use of them before, during and after an event. Pre-event photographs of cars, taken during reconnaissance, were regarded as essential. Feed of news on a "local-boy-makes-good" basis was also important.

It was agreed that such an appointment should be made, subject to the selection of a suitable candidate.

The good work so far done by Miss Ann Clayton should not be disregarded. She might usefully fit into the scheme of things as the main home-based contact.

Apart from Press stories, the provision of posters, following successes, for distribution to Dealers in affected areas, should be examined and pursued.

/6.

Point 3 Motorsport and "ethical and businesslike lines" could be considered a contradiction in terms in some areas today. Point 5 reflects a growing concern that we were not making enough of our efforts. The frustration led to my note to John Thornley on 8.11.63 (see later).

1961 to 1967: THE MIDDLE YEARS by Stuart Turner

-3-

6. **The Ford challenge and our answer.**

Notes were circulated on this problem, and much discussion ensued. It was decided that:

(a) The development of single and twin overhead camshaft, 5-bearing crankshaft, engines, in the A. Series, of 1000 cc. and 1300 cc. should be pursued for use in advanced versions of the Cooper S.

(b) Development should go ahead on a 7-bearing 3-litre power unit for the MGB., possibly using single O.H.C. on an aluminium head. Modifications to the MGB. to accept this engine should proceed in parallel.

Target date for production May 1964.

(NOTE: "This could be done if there were a war on. And this is WAR.")

The existing MGB. rear axle will not accommodate the high ratio which will be necessary. This to be investigated.

7. **Any other business.**

(a) Mr. S. Turner requested that Capital (approximately £2000) be made available for the purchase of a roller dynamometer for Abingdon, and this was agreed.

In the course of the discussion, the Chairman asked why so much competition engine development was carried out at Abingdon. He stressed that the principle must be followed that competition engine development should be conducted by Mr. E. Maher.

(b) Mr. S. Turner stated that it appeared from correspondence that the standard of work carried out by Downton for private owners was markedly inferior to that done by him for B.M.C., and that there was a tendency for the product to be blamed. The Chairman stated that Downton should be told of this, and that it should not continue.

(c) Mr. S. Turner stated that, with the retirement of Miss Carlisle, Mr. Don Moore was left with little to do, and that there was a risk that he would go over to the opposition. He asked that a car be loaned to Mr. Moore for him to develop and tune, and to maintain his interest. Agreed that an MGB. be lent.

JWT/GEVC.
21.10.63.

Point 7a John Cooper had good links to Eddie Maher but, despite this minute, Abingdon continued to do much of its own development. Point 7c I rated Don Moore very highly, as both an engine tuner and a person.

Scale I was a list of events to make enthusiasts' eyes water. Although we were occasionally concerned about the cost of bonus schemes, they remained the best way of placating the countless private owners who wanted to campaign our cars.

SUGGESTED BONUS SCHEME FOR 1964.

Scale I — Monte Carlo, Tulip, Alpine, Liege, Tour de France, R.A.C. and Safari Rallies, together with any race allied to the British Grand Prix.

Scale II — Any races included on the International Calendar (over 100 kilometres long) (excluding National Open events on the SMMT Bond which are at present included), and the following rallies:

Shell 4000 (Canada); Acropolis (Greece); Midnight Sun (Sweden); German (Germany); Polish (Poland); Thousand Lakes (Finland) and Geneva Rally (Switzerland).

Scale III — Any other events which have a full International permit, and any races of up to and including 100 kilometres.

	Scale I	Scale II	Scale III
General Classification			
1st	£ 500	£ 250	£ 75
2nd	200	100	50
3rd	100	50	-
Winning Team or Ladies' Cup	150	50	-
Class Awards			
1st	150	50	30
2nd	75	25	15

To: **Mr. J.W. Thornley**   ST/DMK   From: **S. Turner**
8.11.63

Competition Publicity

We have kept the terms of reference for "Mr. X" so vague that it might be useful to set down some of the avenues of publicity which might be explored.

<u>Television</u> (by far the most difficult but equally the most rewarding)

1. Interviews with our crews on regional feature programmes before and/or after rallies.

2. Film clips (e.g. "Pauline Mayman leaves Paris at the start of the Monte Carlo Rally...") as soon as humanly possible, so that they are topical.

3. Possible "To-night" feature before the Monte (Willy Cave and Raymond Baxter might be our contacts here).

4. When Eric Carlsson won the Monte in 1962, ITV wanted him to fly back for "Sunday Night at the London Palladium". <u>If</u> we ever pulled off an outright, they might play ball.

5. If "What's My Line" comes back (heaven forbid) a professional rally driver should beat the panel. Willy Cave's wife Julia does the research for the programme and some rich Irish dialogue betwixt Eamonn Andrews and Paddy could perhaps give the latter a chance to slip in a BMC plug.

6. Dunlops use GP drivers in tyre ads after major wins; perhaps they could be persuaded to use rally drivers as well. Other companies (I think Bovril ?) have approached Pat Moss in the past and we could perhaps explore this field further.

7. It is probably inevitable that TWTWTW will do a sketch on the Monte Carlo Rally. Perhaps if we supplied it for them, we could make a reference to the Mini that was humorous but kinder than one written by their own writers. (Perhaps a journalist sitting on the beach in Monte typing out deathless prose about rally cars clawing their way through snow and ice).

Mr X was the proposed new PR person in the team – in fact, it became Wilson McComb.
Point 3 My crystal ball was working well because, when we won, they did play ball.
Point 7. With the importance and impact of That Was The Week That Was, *this wasn't quite as daft as it seemed. The comment was triggered by hearing about one doyen of motoring journalism who, after returning from a press trip to try a new car, phoned the manufacturer to ask which country he'd actually visited! His deathless prose began: "As I sat talking to Sheikh so-and-so last night ..."*

Radio

This seems to offer fewer possibilities although Pauline could perhaps be placed on Woman's Hour along the lines of "How a Housewife copes with a Family and the Monte Carlo Rally".

Press

1. Plenty of snippets for "Rally Round-up" and "Track Topics" in Motoring News, "Pit and Paddock" in Autosport, etc.

2. Possible pix of the Morley brothers in Farming magazines, Pauline in women's magazines, etc.

3. Articles for Car Mechanics or Practical Motorist "Preparing your car for rallying", with Mini illustrations.

4. Possible article for Austin Magazine and Motoring on the life of our service cars.

5. Articles on rallying for children's comics (catch the customers when they are young).

6. An annual "Meet the Press" luncheon or cocktail party, either after the R.A.C. or during the Motor Show (to save on Finnish air fares), so that the press can fire questions at our rally team.

7. Investigate the possibility of hiring a forest so that the braver elements of the press can sit with our Mini-Finns on loose going, to study their technique at first hand.

8. Feature stories on private owners, (e.g. Mick Cave with his A 40) who do well in BMC cars.

General

1. Place pictures of our rally cars to illustrate suppliers' stands at the Motor Show and Racing Car Show.

2. Liaison with Finnish Embassy over exploitation of Finnish drivers.

3. We get frequent requests for our drivers to talk to Motor Clubs. Arrange local publicity in such cases.

General 3 It was soon after this that we began running driver forums at dealers and motor clubs.

BMC Competitions Department Secrets ...

Point 5 Reflects the much closer links which existed by then between international and club events. It's great that the BTRDA is still a force in the sport today.

- 3 -

4. Liaise with BMC Geneva and main Continental distributors over publicity. Crews will co-operate <u>provided</u> it is appreciated that they are often tense and busy before a rally.

5. Keep in touch with club motor sport and send out press releases if BT and RDA championships are won in our cars.

6. Mailing list to include motoring correspondents of all evening and weekly papers. Many write under a nom de plume, such as "Marshal", or "King Pin", which will make it easier to keep mailing lists up to date.

7. The Hickey type of column should not be neglected although our society contact, Christabel Carlisle, has now retired. However we do have Sir Peter Moon!

8. Liaison with advertising agents over ads so that they are briefed as to what we <u>might</u> win, and have appropriate pix.

9. Several distributors ask for rally cars for display purposes; someone to co-ordinate this and arrange appropriate backing literature.

Dictated by Mr. Turner and signed in his absence.

E Morley
M-M S2/P1.

MONTE – MONTE TEST 2.
TURINI
!!!! NOTES START AT HOTEL de la POSTE, MOULINET.

<u>HPR</u> 200
<u>HPL</u> 50   F°L 50
<u>HPR</u> 75
F°R 100
L MIN + FR + F°L 50
⊙ FL + <u>LONG FL TIGHTENS</u> + <u>MR</u> 75
F°L + FL + LONG F°R 100
F°R 100 F°L to △ L MIN + F°L + LONG FR 75
KINK LONG FR + F°L 50
△ FL 50 TUNNEL + F°R 75
KINKS FL ᴵᴺᵀᴼ R MIN + HPL + FL +
<u>HPR</u> + F°R 50

(KINK F°L)

The handwriting is mine but these typical pace notes were used by Erle Morley, sitting alongside brother Donald. With the help of all the co-drivers, the system was based on previous work by John Gott and John Sprinzel. We even contacted the Royal Air Force to see if it could help us based on its ground to air communication experience. The RAF couldn't, but felt our scheme was okay. Note the inclusion of kilometre posts, 'A' poles, and road signs here and there to help co-drivers know exactly where they were in, say, heavy snow. I tried to standardise the notes as far as possible so that it would be easier for ice note crews to mark on them the road conditions, but inevitably crews wanted to develop their own methods. The small 'o' over FL and FR here and there was used to quickly upgrade a corner from 'fast left' to 'flat left' if a second practice run suggested this was sensible. Erle has the first note from the next page, on the bottom; a wise precaution in case you fumble when turning over then find the next bend is a hairpin. Pace notes are like sheds in that they should be cleared out every so often otherwise they become unnecessarily complicated.

1961 to 1967: THE MIDDLE YEARS by Stuart Turner

Point 1 The first of two Competitions Committees in 1964 which was mainly concerned with putting pressure on 970 Mini-Cooper production. Point 2(a)(ii) This proposal reflected the ongoing debate about just how much power it was possible to put through the small front wheels of a Mini.

NOTES ON MEETING IN MR. ISSIGONIS' OFFICE 30.7.64.

Present :
Mr. A. Issigonis.
Mr. J.W. Thornley.
Mr. W.V. Appleby.
Mr. A.S. Enever.
Mr. E.J. Maher.
Mr. G.S. Turner.
Mr. Donald Healey.

1. COOPER S.970.

Mr. Thornley outlined the unpleasant and dangerous situation which existed in the motor sporting world because of the non-production of the 970 Cooper S. He stressed that it was desperately important (literally) that outstanding orders should be satisfied immediately and some cars made available in dealers' showrooms.

It was stated that production had been scheduled at 50 per week for eight weeks from this current week. Mr. Appleby stated that some 400 blocks were available. Mr. Maher said he could see 30 engines this week, but crankshafts were the holding factor.

Mr. Issigonis assured the meeting that the heat was full on.

2. FORD CHALLENGE.

In both Saloon Car Racing and Rallying the Ford Cortina now has the edge of the 1300 Coopers, and the Lotus Cortina is way out in front. The Anglia, too, is breathing down the Cooper's neck.

Therefore, a good showing in Saloon Car Racing is no longer possible and outright wins in scratch rallies can only be achieved with a degree of luck which we have no right to expect.

The Lotus Cortina has a racing engine: 1600 cc. over-square, 2 - OHC giving a published 140 h. at 6,5, in a weight of the order of 14 cwt. It must therefore be conceded that we cannot expect to be on equal terms with Ford without a comparable engine. (And this, of course, excludes consideration of the "big bangers" which may be expected to beat Ferrari next year.)

Future plans were discussed against this background with the following results :

(a) Saloon Car Racing.

(i) This should be continued in order to maintain spectator interest, but serious consideration should be given before again entering the Saloon Car Championship.

(ii) A 1-off Mini giving some 135 h.p. would be constructed quickly (? 1270 with 6/7 lbs. boost) to determine the limits of useful power.

(b) Rallying.

(The target here must still be the outright win. Our past successes dictate that class wins can never again be a primary aim.)

(i) We are far from outclassed in handicap rallies (e.g. Monte and Tulip) and the 970 Cooper S. could still finish in the first few.

(ii) In scratch rallies, Touring (saloon) cars would be out classed, except for Class wins. Our main attack must be in the G.T. category though it is, generally speaking, more difficult for a G.T. car to win outright. Our main weapons must continue to be the Austin-Healey 3 000, backed up, where appropriate, by the MGB.

- 2 -

    (iii) With a view to the possible extension of the competitive life of the Austin-Healey 3000, Mr. Maher would complete for comparative test - as a matter of urgency - a 3.2 litre version of the C. series engine using an alloy block and head.

    (iv) In the long term, ADO.51/52 are regarded as the best potential competition vehicles (GT. only). Meantime, additional power for the MGB. should be sought. A 1-off MGB. 5-bearing power unit, de-stroked to 1588 cc. and employing single OHC., would be built for test and car test. Such an engine would be adaptable to ADO.17.

    (v) Extending (iii) above, an ADO.52 engine would be built with an alloy block.

3. **PROGRAMME FOR 1964**.

   (a) *European Rallies*. Agreed that we should enter as last year but excluding Acropolis.

   (b) *Saloon Car Racing*. See Para. 2 (a) (i) above.

   (c) *Safari*. Chances of success in this are now even more remote, but we will undoubtedly be pressed for assistance to local Distributors for flag-flying purposes. Agreed that the Director of Publicity should decide if such requests should be met.

   (d) *Targa Florio*. A rally drivers' circuit, which is coming back into popularity. Agreed to enter two Austin-Healey 3000 rally cars.

   (e) *Sebring*. We must show the flag. Furthermore, the Sprite-Midget must attempt to beat the Spitfires. The following entries were agreed :

    (i) One Sprite and one Midget to be entered as Prototypes. The ex-Jacobs cars may be used for this.

    (ii) BMC/Hambro to be asked if they wish the Qvale exercise to be repeated with MGBs.

    (iii) Donald Healey Motor Co. to enter one Austin-Healey 3000.

NOTE : Drivers in all cases to be approved by us and not nominated by Madison Avenue.

   (f) *Le Mans*. Speed differentials on this circuit become progressively more alarming. Essential that our cars should be as fast as possible; therefore enter in Prototype category to give complete freedom of specification.

    (i) Again the Spitfire must be contained, therefore run one Sprite with 1300 engine.

    (ii) MGB. to run again. If engine of Para." (b) (iv) above is successful, this could be used.

4. **ANY OTHER BUSINESS**.

   (a) Mr. Turner asked if consideration could be given to some Record attempt to take place in an otherwise quiet competition period. He instanced a high-speed, long-distance run with a car which does not normally attract competition publicity, e.g. Wolseley, Riley, Princess,

   (b) A further meeting will be held during the first week of September to consider drivers and their emoluments, publicity and finance.

JWT/GEVC.
4.8.64.

> Point 3(c) The Safari was glamorous and important but we knew we hadn't a winning car for it. There was a conviction then that one needed a local driver to win; it was some years before Hannu Mikkola disabused people of this notion.

1961 to 1967: THE MIDDLE YEARS by Stuart Turner

Although the cars were not festooned with sponsors' details, the team received financial and, more importantly, on-the-ground support from Castrol. Castrol also ran very substantial advertising campaigns about its links with the team.

ITINERAIRE

Spa, Jalhay, Eupen, Hauset, Aachen (Autobahn), Köln (Autobahn), Frankfurt (Autobahn), Karlsruhe (Autobahn), Ulm (Autobahn), Neu-Ulm, Vohringen, Heimertingen, Memmingen, Leutkirch, Lindau, Bregenz, Bludenz, Landeck, Nauders, Passo di Resia, Spondigna, Merano, contourner Bolzano, Ora, Trento, Rovereto, Pian di Fugazze, Passo di Xomo, Posina, Arsiero, Mosson, Tresché-Conca, Asiago, Gallio, Enego, Grigno, Castello Tesino, Passo di Brocon, Ronco, Mezzano, Fiera di Primiero, Passo di Cereda, Don, Agordo, Passo Duran, Villa Dont, Forno di Zoldo, Longarone, Pieve di Cadore, Pelos, Passo di Mauria, Ampezzo, Tolmezzo, Chiusaforte, Pontebba, Tarvisio, Kranjska Gora, Jesenice, Bled, Bohinjska Bistrica, Grahovo, Zelin, Cerkno, Hotavlje, Idrija, Col, Cerknica, Prezid, Osilnica, Brod, Vrbovsko, Carr. Ogulin, Jasenak, Novi, Senj, Brinje, Skradnik, Karlovac, Zagreb, Autoroute, Sl. Brod-Autoroute, Autoroute, Belgrade, Autoroute, Paracin, Zajecar, Kula, Vidin, Belogradcik, Mihajlovgrad, SOFIA, Dimitrovgrad, Pirot, Nis, Kursumlija, Pristina, à proximité de Kos. Mitrovica, Pec, Andrijevica, Matesevo, Lijeva Rijeka, Titograd, Carrefour Kotor, Kotor, Perast, Grahovo, Trebinje, Mrkonjici, Stolac, Tasovcici, Vrgorac, Zagvozd, Sestanovac, Split, Sibenik, Gulin, Bribir, Benkovac, Obrovac, Karlobag, Senj, Novi, Rijeka-Fiume, Ilirska Bistrica, Postojna, Adjovscina, Gorizia, Udine, Codroipo, Pordenone, Vittorio Veneto, Ponte Nelli Alpi, Belluno, Feltré, Primolano, Borgo, Lévico, Trento, Vezzano, Dro, Arco, Riva, Tiarno, Ca Rossa, Lodrone, Bagolino, Croce Domini, Bienno, Cividate, Borno, Croce di Salven, Schilpario, Fondi, Passo di Vivione, Forno d'Allione, Edolo, Ponte di Legno, Passo di Gavia, Bormio, Passo di Stelvio, Trafoi, Gomagoi, Spondigna, Passo di Resia, Nauders, Landeck, Bludenz, Bregenz, Lindau, Leutkirch, Memmingen, Heimertingen, Vohringen, Neu-Ulm, Ulm, Autobahn, Pforzheim-Autobahn, Karlsruhe-Autobahn, Darmstadt-Autobahn, Siegburg-Autobahn, Köln-Autobahn, Aachen-Autobahn, Hauset, Eupen, Jalhay, Spa.

Heures de Fonctionnement des Contrôles

Les heures indiquées ci-dessous se rapportent à l'équipage fictif n° 0.

Chaque équipage trouvera ses heures propres en ajoutant à celles du tableau un nombre de minutes égal à son numéro de départ.

Exemple : le contrôle de Lindau, ouvert de 07 h. 15 à 08 h. 15 pour l'équipage fictif n° 0, le sera de 07 h. 23 à 08 h. 23 pour l'équipage n° 8.

Les heures figurant entre parenthèses s'appliquent à tous les équipages, quel que soit leur numéro de départ.

Les heures de fermeture de ces contrôles de signature sont fixées en prévision d'une participation de 120 voitures. Elles seraient prolongées d'autant de minutes qu'il y aurait de voitures supplémentaires inscrites.

Contrôle	Ouverture	Fermeture
HAUSET (C.H.)	mardi 22 h. 00	à mardi 23 h. 00
NEU ULM (C.H.)	mercredi 05 h. 00	à mercredi 06 h. 00
LINDAU (C.H.)	mercredi 07 h. 15	à mercredi 08 h. 15
PASSO DI RESIA (C.H.)	mercredi 10 h. 45	à mercredi 11 h. 45
PASSO DI XOMO (C.H.)	mercredi 14 h. 15	à mercredi 16 h. 00
Tresche-Conca (C.S.)	(mercredi 14 h. 45	à mercredi 19 h. 15*)
ENEGO (C.H.)	mercredi 15 h. 40	à mercredi 17 h. 40
Passo di Brocon (C.S.)	(mercredi 16 h. 15	à mercredi 21 h. 00*)
VILLA DONT (C.H.)	mercredi 17 h. 45	à mercredi 20 h. 15
BLED (C.H.)	mercredi 21 h. 30	à jeudi 00 h. 30
Grahovo (C.S.)	(mercredi 22 h. 00	à jeudi 03 h. 30*)
Hotavlje (C.S.)	(mercredi 22 h. 30	à jeudi 04 h. 15*)
COL (C.H.)	mercredi 23 h. 30	à jeudi 02 h. 30
CARREFOUR OGULIN (C.H.)	jeudi 01 h. 40	à jeudi 04 h. 40
NOVI (C.H.)	jeudi 02 h. 40	à jeudi 05 h. 40
Brinje (C.S.)	(jeudi 03 h. 00	à jeudi 09 h. 00*)
ZAGREB (C.H.)	jeudi 05 h. 30	à jeudi 08 h. 30
SL. BROD-Autobahn (C.H.)	jeudi 07 h. 30	à jeudi 10 h. 30
BELGRADE (C.H.)	jeudi 09 h. 30	à jeudi 12 h. 30
BELOGRADCIK (C.H.)	jeudi 13 h. 15	à jeudi 16 h. 15
SOFIA (C.H.)	jeudi 15 h. 45	à jeudi 18 h. 45
KURSUMLIJA (C.H.)	jeudi 19 h. 45	à jeudi 22 h. 45
PEC (C.H.)	jeudi 22 h. 20	à vendredi 01 h. 20
Lijeva Rijeka (C.S.)	(vendredi 00 h. 00	à vendredi 05 h. 30*)
TITOGRAD (C.H.)	vendredi 01 h. 00	à vendredi 04 h. 00
Carrefour Kotor (C.S.)	(vendredi 01 h. 50	à vendredi 07 h. 20*)
PERAST (C.H.)	vendredi 02 h. 30	à vendredi 05 h. 30
STOLAC (C.H.)	vendredi 04 h. 30	à vendredi 07 h. 30
Zagvozd (C.S.)	(vendredi 05 h. 30	à vendredi 11 h. 15*)
SPLIT (C.H.)	vendredi 06 h. 45	à vendredi 09 h. 45
Bribir (C.S.)	(vendredi 07 h. 45	à vendredi 13 h. 30*)
OBROVAC (C.H.)	vendredi 09 h. 00	à vendredi 14 h. 00
NOVI (C.H.)	vendredi 11 h. 15	à vendredi 14 h. 00
ADJOVSCINA (C.H.)	vendredi 13 h. 30	à vendredi 16 h. 00
VITTORIO VENETO (C.H.)	vendredi 16 h. 15	à vendredi 18 h. 15
BORGO (C.H.)	vendredi 18 h. 30	à vendredi 20 h. 00
BAGOLINO (C.H.)	vendredi 21 h. 00	à vendredi 22 h. 00
BIENNO (C.H.)	vendredi 21 h. 45	à vendredi 22 h. 45
SCHILPARIO (C.H.)	vendredi 22 h. 30	à vendredi 23 h. 30
Forno d'Allione (C.N.)	vendredi 22 h. 45	à samedi 00 h. 30
Ponte di Legno (C.N.)	vendredi 23 h. 45	à samedi 01 h. 30
TRAFOI (C.H.)	samedi 01 h. 15	à samedi 02 h. 15
PASSO DI RESIA (C.H.)	samedi 02 h. 00	à samedi 03 h. 00
LINDAU (C.H.)	samedi 05 h. 30	à samedi 06 h. 30
NEU ULM (C.H.)	samedi 08 h. 00	à samedi 09 h. 00
PFORZHEIM-Autobahn (C.H.)	samedi 09 h. 30	à samedi 10 h. 30
DARMSTADT-Autobahn (C.H.)	samedi 11 h. 15	à samedi 12 h. 15
SIEGBURG-Autobahn (C.H.)	samedi 13 h. 25	à samedi 14 h. 25
HAUSET (C.H.)	samedi 15 h. 00	à samedi 16 h. 00
SPA (C.H.)	samedi 15 h. 30	à samedi 16 h. 30

— 7 —

I'm sorry if this section has an over-emphasis on the Liège, but not very, because, in my book, it was the toughest and the greatest of them all. This is the list of controls for the 1964 event.

1961 to 1967: THE MIDDLE YEARS by Stuart Turner

And this is how those controls look on a map. Driving an A110 service car, I arrived at Belgrade to find crowds lining the street, not for the rally but an international conference. The police thought the A110 meant a visiting dignitary, so we were waved through ahead of all the other traffic. Not many years ago I saw TV footage of a tank parked where we used to set up service on the rally …

Date: 25-29 AUGUST Event: LIEGE - SOFIA - LIEGE 1964. Cat. & Group: 4.

MAKINEN - BARROW.

Car Type	Engine No.	Chassis No.	Comp. No.	Mechanic
A/H 3000. ARX 92 B				S. MOYLAN.

Cylinder Block

Bore size	+ .040
Modified	Cut valve recess
Fume pipes	STD
Camshaft	704/539 FIT NEW
Crankshaft	Balanced EN 40 nitrated (fit plugs) FIT NEW
Flywheel	SPL 20 lbs. 8 bolt fixing
Clutch	SPL 9½" diaphragm
Release bearing	STD 13H.822
Bearings cam	STD
Bearings crank	SPL Vandervell
Con rods	STD balanced
Pistons	STD + .040"
Oil pump	STD
Oil pump drive	STD
Camshaft gear	704/530
Crankshaft gear	STD
Timing chain	STD
Core plugs	Fit retainers
Dip stick & washer	Blued
Oil filter element	STD
Distributor	STD (RT)
Ignition setting	6° BTDC static
Engine rubbers	SPL hardened
Check Engine No. Plate	/
Idler gear	Nil
Primary gear	Nil
Oil pressure	Check
Sump & protection	Large capacity. Full sump shield
Sump plug	Modified
Oil cooler	Nil

Part of the build sheet for an Austin-Healey 3000 for the '64 Liège.

1961 to 1967: THE MIDDLE YEARS by Stuart Turner

Liège 1964.   Instructions for Service Crews

General Points

1. Study these instructions carefully. Plans for all service crews are included so that you can tell where everyone will be at a given time.

2. Service crews at petrol stops must watch the danger of fire, particularly from spectators with cigarettes.

3. The Liege this year is not a rally; it is a thinly disguised road race and many service points will be virtually pit stops if the crews are not to lose time. If a car is in trouble and <u>has</u> to stay at one of these points while work is done <u>leave it the moment a later number arrives</u> and send that on its way before returning to the sick car.

4. There will not be many finishers this year (the Organisers think about 7 !) so there may well be some broken cars to bring back. Once you have finished your final service point it is therefore imperative that you carefully carry out the rest of your instructions to liaise with other service crews in "sweeping up".

5. Some service cars must have a supply of "results pads" to give details to the crews after phoning Liege. When phoning Liege give Peter Browning any snippets of information that you may have about the rally so that this can be passed on to London and thence to the press.

6. All cars will have a supply of long-lasting bread. Keep sandwiches as moist as possible and have glucose drinks for the crews (prepare these even where they theoretically will have no time - they might just be able to grab a drink or sandwich to take with them.) Have the drinks prepared in sufficient quantity to refill flasks. Locally grown melons seem popular with some of the crews.

7. If you are at a point where they are likely to have over 20 minutes try to find a hotel room where crews can wash; if you are servicing in the middle of the dust and crews have only a minute or two, duck their heads under a tap if one is available.

8. <u>Dont</u> rely on hotels to wake you if you have to service in the early hours - take an alarm clock.

Service Crews & Equipment are as follows:

6/110	S. Turner, G. Wiffen, P. Bartram with one spare wheel, one full kit, one emergency kit, 8 petrol bags and a funnel (in a grip or suitcase for P. Bartram to take by air)
Traveller & trailer	D. Watts, J. Organ, R. Brocklehurst with 100 gallon tankage, a pump, a funnel, one full kit and 1 spare wheel. (J. Simpson of Castrol should be given an emergency kit for when J. Organ joins him).
Traveller	T. Wellman, B. Moylan, P. Easter, with one full kit, one spare wheel, one emergency kit for B. Moylan and 16 bags and a funnel.
Traveller	B. Hancock, G. Barritt, M. Norton with 100 gallon tankage, a pump, a funnel, one spare wheel, plenty of rope and a strong bar.
A110 & trailer	D. Green, M. Poole, D. Hayter with 100 gallon container, a pump, a funnel, one spare wheel, one full kit and one emergency kit for M. Poole.
A110	W.R. Price, T. Eales with one full kit, one spare wheel, some soap and a bag of clothes per driver.
MG 1100	F. Cooper, R. Whittington, with one full kit and a bag of clean clothes per driver.

<u>N.B.</u> All service crews must carry 2 spare tubes and a 4 gall. bag for their own cars. (Have the bag filled at each service point in case anyone is short).

Just one of several pages of team instructions for the Liège. Point 3 "... thinly disguised road race..."; "... pit stops ..." – is it any wonder people still drool at the name Liège?

Point 7 I managed to find a pump at one service point on an earlier Liège and ducked a few heads under it – including John Gott's who was then a Chief Constable. Happy days ... We had a special 100 gallon rubber bag made in which fuel was towed across Yugoslavia. We came round a corner in the 6/110 to find John Wadsworth and Mike Wood parked in their Mini-Cooper with – what else? – a broken coupling. We weren't officially carrying spares for them but, to my surprise, mechanic Pete Bartram calmly pulled out a spare he'd slipped into his toolbox; they went on to finish 20th, the only time a Mini finished the event.

BMC Competitions Department Secrets ...

```
                    COMPETITION REPORT

Type of car      A.H.3000                  Reg.No. BMO 93 B
Event            Spa-Sofia-Liege 1964
Driver           R. Aaltonen
Crew             T. Ambrose
Mileage out    )
Mileage in     )  Don't know
Distance covered)
```

1. ENGINE PERFORMANCE

Power satisfactory?	Excellent
Carburation satisfactory?	Excellent
Ignition satisfactory?	Excellent
Petrol consumption?	Normal
Oil consumption?	Normal
Grade of oil?	XL
Oil pressure variation?	80 - 55 lb/sq. in.
Max. revs used?	6,000
Any excessive pinking or running-on experienced?	No
Any work carried out?	No
Any other comment or suggestion	A fantastic engine, still giving an excellent power output at the finish.

2. TRANSMISSION

Noise in any gear?	Ok
Final drive noise?	Ok
Lever vibration?	Ok
Oil leakage?	Nil
Ease of change?	Good
Clutch satisfactory?	Yes
Any other comment or suggestion	Overdrive unreliable in early stages due to electrical fault, but in spite of lack of optimism after work by BMC and later by Laycocks, this gave no trouble during second half of event

3. ROADHOLDING

How was the general balance of the car?	Excellent
Was the steering light and did it remain so?	Yes
Was the steering sufficiently accurate at all speeds?	Yes
Was there any steering wheel shake, wheel patter or axle tramp?	No
Type of tyres fitted?	U.K. SP's on tarmac, German SP's on loose
What was the tyre wear and what pressures?	Excessive at rear 26F 28 - 30 R
Any shock absorber trouble?	Yes, both rears failed by ¾ distance. One replaced by spare from Makinens car but this also failed
Any suspension rattles?	No
Any other comment or suggestion	Bump rubbers failed before half distance. It would have been better had these been replaced at Sofia as a matter of policy. See General Summary concerning tyre wear

4. BRAKING

Brake material used?	D.S.11 front and rear
Did you experience brake fade and under what conditions?	No
Were brakes fierce or pulling to one side?	No
Did you lose the pedal through any cause?	Not excessively
How often did you adjust the brakes?	Twice
Were they noisy?	No
Any other comment or suggestion	

5. ELECTRICAL SYSTEM

Was the lighting satisfactory?	Excellent
Did you have any fanbelt or dynamo troubles?	No
Did you make any electrical repairs or replacements?	Horns failed, but were repaired using spares from Makinens car
Was consumption of battery fluid excessive?	Normal
Any other comment or suggestion	Very reliable

(This page and opposite) Crews were asked to complete report forms after every event. This is Tony Ambrose's for the winning 3000 on the '64 Liège. Note the comment in point 9 about tyre wear.

1961 to 1967: THE MIDDLE YEARS by Stuart Turner

6. BODY

Were there any leaks or draughts?	Best 3000 yet built
Was the seating comfortable?	Excellent. The importance of a high seating for this type of event, cannot be over-emphasised
Did any body furniture break or prove uncomfortable or unsatisfactory?	Window winders need very careful padding on new model. Knee pads should extend well back on nearside door
Were the pedals and/or gear lever properley positioned?	Yes
Were the switches and minor controls in easy places?	Yes
Was the visibility satisfactory?	Yes
Did the screen wipers and washers work satisfactorily?	Yes
Was the heating, demisting and ventilation effective?	No, it was necessary to impossible to produce a blower for windscreen for A.H.3000 and possibility of using Mini Cooper blower unit for all competition 3000's should be investigated
Were the instruments accurate, visible and well lit at nights?	Yes
Any other comment or suggestion	Hard-top came loose in spite of suspension fixing to previous years even more attention must be paid to this

7. PREPARATION

Was the car handed over to you in good condition?	Excellent
Were the tools, spares and equipment sufficient and satisfactory?	Yes
Were the servicing arrangements during the event adequate?	Yes
Any other comment or suggestion	

8. CHOICE OF CAR

Do you consider ther is a better BMC car for the event?	No
How did your car compare with its rally or commercial competitors?	We won
Any other comment or suggestion	

9. GENERAL SUMMARY OF THE CAR'S PERFORMANCE, LIKES, DISLIKES AND COMMENTS.

A fantastic car prepared with the utmost attention to necessary detail as well as to fundamental components.

The rate of wear of rear tyres was fantastic. We just managed to scrape through from Bled to Col, Col to Novi and Pec to Stolac, but could have been in trouble on these sections had we had a puncture and if service cars had not been carrying a minimum of two spares which we took. Had the other 3000's been doing well in the latter stages this could have been embarrassing.

Tony Ambrose.

BMC Competitions Department Secrets ...

B.M.C. COMPETITIONS COMMITTEE.

MINUTES OF MEETING HELD IN MR. G.W. HARRIMAN'S OFFICE AT LONGBRIDGE ON 4TH SEPTEMBER 1964.

Present:
    Mr. G.W. Harriman.
    Mr. A. Issigonis.
    Mr. J.W. Thornley.
    Mr. G.S. Turner.

1. The notes on the meeting held by Mr. Issigonis on 30th July were considered and approved, subject to the following comments :

(a) <u>Mini-Cooper S.970.</u>

It was confirmed that some 260 of these had been produced to date and that production would continue at a steady rate until 1,000 had been completed. Mr. Suffield had confirmed that he had order cover for over 1,000. It was agreed that the balance of this 1,000 would be produced with normal suspension.

In the course of the meeting Mr. Harriman requested Mr. Suffield to send three cars each to Woodhouse and Bruggemann as a matter of urgency.

(b) <u>Ford Challenge.</u>

(i) It was agreed that we should re-enter the Saloon Car Championship for 1965.

(ii) Downton should be asked to develop a 1270 Mini engine to produce 135 h.p.

(iii) Mr. Issigonis would urge the development of the MGB. 5-bearing power unit on the lines of Note 2 (b) (iv).

(c) <u>Programme for 1964.</u>

(i) <u>Sebring.</u>

Mr. Thornley would write to Mr. Qvale to see if he was prepared to undertake the running of the MGB.s at Sebring, as was done last year.

Mr. Harriman agreed with Mr. C. Healey's suggestion that two Sprites and two Midgets should run.

Selection of drivers would be controlled from England to ensure adequate driving ability, as distinct from personal publicity value.

(ii) <u>Le Mans.</u>

Two Sprites with 1300 engines would be run, and one MGB.

(iii) <u>East African Safari.</u>

An ADO.17 and ADO.16 would be run by the Competitions Department, first in Wales, then, if they displayed suitable potential, on reconnaissance in Africa.

(iv) It was agreed that we should enter the Vultava Rally in Czecho-Slovakia.

(v) 24-hour Touring Race at Spa to be entered.

(vi) <u>Record-breaking.</u>

The possibility of this to be investigated. An event should be organised on a wide B.M.C. basis, e.g. ADO.15, 16, 17 and 6/110, displaying progressive performance.

/2.

The final Competitions Committee of 1964. Whether because of problems besetting the company, or because people trusted us more, I don't know, but the Committee had shrunk in size for this meeting. Not that I was complaining. Point 1(a) The request to send cars on the Continent was to help give the impression the 970 was out and about. Point 1(c) iii ADO 16 = Austin/Morris 1100/1300s. ADO 17 = Austin/Morris 1800s

1961 to 1967: THE MIDDLE YEARS by Stuart Turner

-2-

2. Drivers for 1965.

(a) Mr. Stuart Turner was given freedom to negotiate within the framework of suggested ceiling figures, as now indicated on the attached budget.

(b) In the course of these negotiations he would endeavour to restrict the Scandinavian drivers to B.M.C. cars.

(c) While the limitations of our existing ladies' crew were appreciated, Mr. Harriman stressed the importance of having a ladies crew. While it might be necessary to drop Mrs. Mayman for the ensuing year, we should keep our eyes wide open for future candidates.

If, as seemed probable in these circumstances, Miss Domleo elected to navigate for Saab with Mrs. Carlsson in 1965, it was agreed we should be liberal in our attitude to requests from her for time off in which to compete.

(d) It was agreed that Aaltonen, Ambrose and Hopkirk, should be sent to fulfil the invitations from Siam di Tella to participate in the Argentine Touring Grand Prix and from B.M.C. (Australia) for the Sandown Park meeting. In the case of Aaltonen and Ambrose this trip would be offered as recognition for the winning of the Spa-Sofia-Liege.

3. Budget for 1964/5.

This was agreed by Mr. Harriman, as attached to these minutes, and as amended to cover the increased figures for drivers' retainers.

4. Other Matters.

(a) **Bonus Scheme.**

For 1965 we would publish our own list of events against which bonus would be paid in the event of private owners' successes.

(b) **Ford Competition News.**

"Safety Fast" was considered as the basis of the reply to this. Mr. Thornley explained the difficult position in which this magazine found itself by virtue of the policy imposed by B.M.C. Service that only items of extra equipment which they handled should be advertised. Mr. Harriman agreed that this embargo be lifted, and that the publication be suitably modified to convey competition news with at least the topicality of the Ford News Sheet, though retaining the present higher quality.

(c) **Transporters.**

It was agreed that negotiations could be opened with John Cooper when the time came that B.M.C. Service were ready to dispose of the first of their mobile service school workshops.

(d) **Competition Service cars.**

Mr. Harriman was not in favour of the use of conversions by outside firms for this purpose. He stated, however, that there was at Vanden Plas a prototype Princess shooting brake which was no longer required, and that this could be taken over by the Competitions Department.

(e) **Police Rally.**

We should continue to support this. Every effort should be made to ensure that our cars were handled by the best available drivers.

(f) **Petrol.**

It was agreed that Mr. Thornley should draft a letter for Mr. Harriman to send to Mr. John Davies, of Shell, outlining the present situation, and requesting advice and assistance.

JWT/GEVC.
8.9.64.

Point 4(b) One advantage of having the Chairman on the Committee was that relatively minor matters like this could be solved in a second. Note the ongoing obsession with what Ford was up to.
Point 4(d) Having this Princess shooting brake at Abingdon was the closest I've ever got to running a Rolls.

BMC Competitions Department Secrets ...

B.M.C. COMPETITIONS COMMITTEE.
COMPETITION BUDGET 1964/65.
(Addendum to Minutes of Meeting 4.9.64).

	£.	£.
Main International Rallies :-		
Spa-Sofia-Liege		10,000
Tour-de-France		9,000
R.A.C.		8,000
Monte Carlo		15,000
Tulip		5,000
Alpine		9,000
		56,000
Sundry Events :-		
Sebring		6,000
Le-Mans		4,000
Targo - Florio		4,000
Individual Entries (i.e. Austrian Alpine, Midnight Sun etc.)		5,000
		75,000
Retainers to Team Drivers :-		
P. Hopkirk	5,000	
R. Aaltonen	4,000	
T. Makinen	3,000	
J.A. Ambrose (6 @ £300)	1,800	
D. Morley (4 @ £400)	1,600	
E. Morley (4 @ £400)	1,600	
H. Liddon (6 @ £250)	1,500	
D. Barrow (6 @ £100)	600	19,100
Support for Private Owners		5,000
Bonus Payments		3,500
Contingencies		5,000
Overheads - Departmental		35,000
Depreciation		5,000
Development		5,000
		152,600
North America		25,000
		£177,600
Healey Competition Programme		**£25,000**

The budget for the Monte was higher than the Liège, partly because of hotel costs in Monaco: there was barely time for hotels on the Liège. Retainers were negotiated by me on an ad hoc basis, influenced, of course, by what overtures were being made by other teams at the time.

1961 to 1967: THE MIDDLE YEARS by Stuart Turner

SILVERSTONE 4.11.64

RACE 3000		RALLY 3000		SPRITE	
Makinen	1.52.0	Makinen	1.55.2	Makinen	1.56.2
Banks	1.52.2	Aaltonen	2.00.2	Aaltonen	1.57.0
Fitzpatrick	1.53.6	Kallstrom	2.00.2	Kallstrom	1.57.0
Mac	1.53.6			Baker	1.58.2
Baker	1.55.8			Fitzpatrick	2.00.6
Aaltonen	1.56.2				
Kallstrom	1.58.4				

MGB		HYDRA MINI		ZF MINI	
Stewart	1.53.2	Stewart	2.00.4	Hopkirk	1.56.4
Hopkirk	1.53.8	Hopkirk	2.00.6	Banks	1.56.8
Aaltonen	1.54.0	Banks	2.01.0	Stewart	1.57.4
Banks	1.54.2	Fitzpatrick	2.01.4	Makinen	1.58.0
Makinen	1.54.4	Aaltonen	2.01.8	Fitzpatrick	1.58.2
Kallstrom	1.54.4	Makinen	2.01.8	Aaltonen	1.59.0
Fitzpatrick	1.55.4	Kallstrom	2.03.2		
Baker	1.55.6				

S/C MINI		OLD MINI		F3	
Banks	1.59.0	Hopkirk	2.00.8	Stewart	1.44.4
Hopkirk	1.59.8	Banks	2.01.0	Mac	1.45.4
Fitzpatrick	2.00.4	Makinen	2.01.0	Banks	1.46.6
Stewart	2.00.6	Kallstrom	2.01.4	Fitzpatrick	1.47.4
Makinen	2.04.2	Stewart	2.01.8		
		Fitzpatrick	2.02.0		
		Jopson	2.02.4		
		Aaltonen	2.02.6		
		Mac	2.03.4		

To assist with driver selection for Sebring, we used to take a variety of cars and drivers to Silverstone for a test day. These are the times as logged by Peter Browning for the test we did on 4.11.64. It was always very convenient to have a skilled timekeeper working at Abingdon! Geoff Healey brought a Sprite along and kept opening the bonnet after every driver. When I asked why at the end of the day, he quietly showed me the extra rev counter he had tucked away … with a tell-tale. So when the lads were claiming "Only 6000 Geoff", he knew different.

This 1962 letter indicates how we were trying to keep to one basic set of pace notes for everyone – works and semi-works cars – so that, as mentioned here, we could feed them back with ice notes marked on them. My very rude final sentence suggests that at the time we were placing more importance on the Hydrolastic Mini than it really warranted.

TELEPHONE: ABINGDON 251
TELEGRAMS: EMGEE, ABINGDON

CHEQUES PAYABLE TO
THE M.G. CAR CO. LTD.

THE BRITISH MOTOR CORPORATION

Competitions Department

ABINGDON-ON-THAMES, BERKSHIRE

John Wadsworth.

(2 copies of each)

Herewith : your pace notes for the tests, when you get back I want one copy back marked with your name (on each sheet) and with any corrections. Take the other copy on the rally with you. The copy you return to us will be given to you at intervals with ice notes marked on. Geoff Mabbs already has his notes and must do the same.

Also enclosed : navigation notes from here to Monte which are **not** accurate compared to 'official route in France' on final run in to Chambery. Also enclosed notes for mountain circuit for you and Geoff.

It is essential that you maintain contact with us so that you link up with Paddy to swop cars so that he can try the Hydro car which you pick up from Nice. If either you or Geoff shunt the Hydro car before you meet Paddy, don't bother phoning us – just chuck yourself in the harbour because your rally career will be over.

And the best of luck.

AUSTIN • AUSTIN-HEALEY • M.G. • MORRIS • RILEY • WOLSELEY

The idea for this success ad, run mid-65, was triggered by a press release Wilson McComb issued highlighting the 65 wins in '65 theme.

1961 to 1967: THE MIDDLE YEARS by Stuart Turner

S Turner

A G E N D A
and
NOTES for
COMPETITIONS COMMITTEE MEETING ON 13TH AUGUST 1965.

1. Drivers for 1966.

It is suggested that we still further condense the team to the three star drivers, Hopkirk, Makinen and Aaltonen. The Morley Brothers may be used in addition, in the event of clashing dates. (Spot car)

Hopkirk is committed to us under the two-year agreement made a year ago, at a fee of £5,000 per annum.

Aaltonen is not committed, but in the current year has received £6,000, plus £50 per start.

Makinen receives £400 per start.

Not unnaturally other manufacturers are nibbling.

Stuart Turner goes to Finland this week-end, and would welcome guidance, with a view to settling with these latter two.

Get best deal

2. Programme for 1966.

The pattern of international events has been changing, such that the only classic rallies now remaining are the Monte, the Alpine and the R.A.C. It is felt that we should continue the policy which has evolved during the current year, where one or two cars are entered in a variety of rallies which, while of international status in the calendar, are primarily of national significance, e.g. Swedish, Circuit of Ireland, Geneva, Czech, German, Polish, etc.

The programme should be left flexible, so that we may meet the enemy on ground of our own choosing, but we would welcome general guidance from the Sales Division to indicate those countries where publicity boost would have greatest advantage.

Some particular events need special consideration :

(a) Bridgehampton, U.S.A. and Australia.

A request has been received from B.M.C./Hambro that we should send drivers to participate with their cars in the Race Meeting at Bridgehampton on 18th September.

B.M.C. Australia have requested that our drivers should participate with their cars in the Armstrong 500 on the 3rd October, and should be available for a P.R. exercise in connection with the announcement in Australia of the 1800 which precedes this Race Meeting. (then do a rally)

These exercises could be achieved for the cost of the air fares.

They pay for car + drivers. Australia pays air fares. +1 MCC + N.Z

(b) East African Safari.

We have never felt that we have the right sort of vehicle to cope with this rally, but Gailey & Roberts are very keen that we should cover it with the 1800. Is this vehicle considered to be strong enough ?

Yes but NO.

(c) Rallye dei Fiori.

This is the leading event in Italy, and the B.M.C. Factory Representative has strongly recommended that we send one or two cars. The event occurs in February, and should we win the Monte for the third time, driver and car could conveniently go on to participate. Otherwise, we would not recommend participation in the absence of a strong recommendation from the Sales Division.

Innocenti? to share cost.

/(d)

T. Write letter to A. Issigonis signature

Point 1 As my note, scribbled when in the meeting, indicates, it was left to me to negotiate the best deals with the drivers.

Point 2 Requesting guidance from the Sales Division a year or so later, when we had to go behind the Iron Curtain for one event to score points, actually contributed to my departure from BMC. When I mentioned we were thinking of using an Austin 1800 for an event, the Sales Chief said: "Oh, you'd help us if you can get Alec to alter the handbrake because customers don't like it." I pointed to the Issigonis office and asked: "Why don't you tell him?" Answer: "Oh, he won't listen to Sales!" I think I must have sensed at that point that the writing was on the wall.

Point 2(b) I think my scribble here means "yes", we understood their keenness, but "no" we weren't going to go.

Point 2(c) We must have been getting more (or over?) confident to suggest we might win the Monte for a third time.

-2-

(d) **Rallye des Cimes.**

At the request of B.M.C. Geneva, we observed this event this year, which is for cross-country vehicles. Whilst in this, its first year, there were only fourteen entries, it attracted considerable publicity in France. It is to be considered whether we send a Gypsy, and possibly a Mini-Moke, in 1966.

(e) **Sports Car Racing.**

To be considered whether we follow a similar pattern as this year at e.g. Sebring, Le Mans, Targa Florio, and possibly Daytona.

(f) **Saloon Car Racing.**

Mr. John Cooper will report on the past year's activities and future intentions.

(g) **Record-breaking, or special events.**

The last Competitions Committee Meeting gave birth to the "Round the World" idea. Is this to be considered still dormant through 1966?

3. **Vehicles.**

F.I.A. regulations covering grouping of cars for competitions have changed radically from January 1st. In place of the two categories which have existed so far -

(i) **Touring,** for which 1,000 examples had to be manufactured for homologation, and

(ii) **Grand Touring,** for which the requirement was 100,

each of these two categories is now sub-divided. The touring category has one section in which the requirement is 5,000, and which must run absolutely in accordance with catalogue, and another of 1,000 where certain modifications are permitted. Grand Touring is similarly sub-divided into manufacturing requirements of 500 and 50. In the case of the Grand Touring car there are moreover now minimum standards of body accommodation.

Of our principal rally-winning vehicles :

(a) The Austin-Healey 3,000 must now be considered as virtually at the end of its long rally career, not only because some of the opposition is now faster, but also because its body does not conform to the minimum requirements of the regulations. It is recommended that consideration should be given to the production of a run of 50 special sports cars which could :-

(i) Finish well up in sports car events.

(ii) Win Alpine rallies and the rougher events where the small Mini wheels are a handicap.

(iii) Do well in American racing.

It is suggested that such a car be based on the ADO.52, the aim being a vehicle with 220 b.h.p. in 16 cwt.

(b) The 1275 Mini-Cooper S. no longer has undisputed command, but can still win rallies outright if entries are selective.

Under the new regulations, however, it is essential that the standard production version of this vehicle should incorporate twin fuel tanks, 1½" carburetters, an oil cooler, and 4½ J. wheels.

In order to avoid accusations of cheating, it is essential that the inboard metal couplings now being used on the competition cars be listed as "export options" for rough markets, and that there are at least some available for general sale.

/4.

2(d) It wasn't until I moved to Ford that I came across the Rallye des Cimes again. We sent a Formula Ford to Ford US in exchange for a Bronco. Rod Chapman ventured off on the rally with the latter ... and came back because it was too wide to go through some of the gates.

Point 2(g) I think you will sense the relief in my additional note signifying the end of any round-the-world ideas.

Point 3(b) The "export options" reflected a common ruse at the time to list things for export markets, although whether any parts were ever sold there is another matter. I always felt it would be possible to get a part listed for sale in a non-existent country, but I was never brave enough to try it.

1961 to 1967: THE MIDDLE YEARS by Stuart Turner

-3-

4. **North American competition.**

No great use appears to have been made of the special cars prepared in accordance with the decision at the last Competitions Committee Meeting for North America, where they would have to compete on level terms with cars of four times the price. Our feeling is that these markets could best be served by the operation of a bonus scheme for private owners similar to that which we operate from Abingdon for the rest of the world, and indeed similar to that which Standard-Triumph operate in the U.S.A. This should be supplemented by a B.M.C./Hambro, or other service van, at race meetings.

There has been a strong application from Mr. Pocock for Canada to be dealt with separately from the U.S.A.

Mr. Suffield's views are sought on these points.

[handwritten margin: LS surprised — bonus scheme not working; LS in favour of bonus scheme] *[handwritten: ALSO]*

5. **Special Tuning Department.**

This is the department set up at the request of B.M.C. Service to handle the sale of special competition components which they did not wish to handle, and to undertake the special tuning of competition cars for the home and export trade. The business of this department is growing satisfactorily, and is beginning to show a margin of profit. It has, however, brought upon itself an enormous volume of customer correspondence seeking tuning advice, which generates an overhead cost which is taking the gilt off the gingerbread.

Since the visit of Mr. Willey, of Longbridge, supplies of this special material have improved somewhat, but there is a substantial back-log of orders, and more co-operation from other departments within B.M.C. in obtaining limited-run items would be appreciated.

6. **Monte Carlo Rally.**

Our effort to pull off the hat trick must be concentrated and dedicated. We therefore renew our annual plea that no-one should give any undertaking to loan a vehicle to Press, policemen, or other fellow travellers, who have little or no chance of winning, and yet would tend to clog our organisation on the ground. A resolution to this effect would be very much appreciated.

[handwritten margin: No-one save Baxter]

7. **Advertising.**

Whilst it is most encouraging to everybody concerned to see competition successes advertised so lavishly, could not consideration be given to linking this advertising more closely with general sales policy with a view to broadening its impact?

[signature]

[handwritten: Liege; how?]

[handwritten: Press Office in our budget.]

JWT/GEVC.
11.8.65.

Point 4 America was always important as a sports car market, which is why it keeps cropping up in these documents. Lester Suffield's views were sought because he had recently returned from running BMC's North American operation. My written addition suggests he supported bonus schemes.

Point 5 The first Committee reference to the Special Tuning Department. As we'd shifted to fewer, more developed cars for our works entries, the old close relationships we'd had with private owners no longer applied. Special Tuning proved a good solution. Inevitably, at the time there were dreams – just as there were later at Ford – that we could sell enough parts to fund a full motorsport programme. Sadly, they were pipe dreams.

Point 6 I put this on the agenda to help me say "no" to the oddball pleas from drivers or supporters that tended to come up for the Monte. My written note refers to Raymond Baxter who was to be an exception to the rule, not just because of his BBC work but because it was good to have him in a team. When we were experimenting with Triplex on heated windscreens, Raymond was the one to spot why drivers seemed slightly slower in one car: the gold film in the screen was impairing vision.

It's not until writing this caption that I realised the irony of the headline to this November 1965 ad ... with Finnish drivers first and second.

1961 to 1967: THE MIDDLE YEARS by Stuart Turner

S. Turner
Competitions Manager

Mr. A.A. Issigonis,
Austin Motor Co. Ltd.,
Longbridge,
Birmingham.

10th January, 1966.

Highly Confidential - read then burn!

Problems with tyre supplies have prevented me coming up to Longbridge to discuss the modifications done to our rally cars. Just in case I am not able to make it before leaving for the rally, the attached list covers all the doubtful items. As I see it, provided there is documentary evidence (preferably with a 1965 date!) that items 1, 2, 3, 5 and 9 have been put in production, we should be all right with these items.

However strict the scrutineering is, it is unlikely to show up items 4 and 6.

Item 8 is already covered and is in production. No details of the oil cooler pipes are listed on the homologation form, so item 10 does not matter. Item 11 is covered by the homologation form while we understand that item 12 is in fact the latest production specification; excepting of course the red units and these are covered by the homologation form anyway. (Incidentally it would be just as well if they could be listed somewhere for some export market!)

According to the drivers, item 7 certainly appears to have solved our immediate suspension problems. Can these therefore be given approval of some sort before the rally ends? I would suggest they be sold through Special Tuning.

Of all the above, the one most likely to attract attention is item 5 and it is imperative that any Coopers made from now on have this specification.

Inclusion of this note and the next may upset some purists, but the comments in them simply reflect what happened back then; other manufacturers were up to similar things. As it turned out, after the Monte disqualification over lighting, a standard car taken from the dealer showroom in Monaco was actually quicker than a rally car.

Confidential

Modifications done to Rally Coopers

1. Bush changed in bottom wishbone arm (see memo from W.J. Daniels of 10th November 1965 recommending universal adoption for Mini range).

2. Support shaft modified for lower wishbone (see memo from W.J. Daniels of 10th November recommending its adoption for Cooper 'S' and Mokes).

3. Remote control mounting changed (see memo from W.J. Daniels of 10th November recommending its adoption on Cooper 'S').

4. Vandervell bush incorporated in primary gear (we have borrowed 24 of these from Downtons which can be held at Engines pending spot inspection by rally scrutineer).

5. Latest drive shaft couplings with modified drive shafts with enlarged bell ends modified suroclip (believed to be the latest Cooper specification - how far off general availability is it?)

6. Timkin bearings used in rear hubs.

7. Sprite/MGB Aeon bump stops fitted on the rear.

8. AEG 510 camshaft (which incidentally shows up well on the rollers).

9. Double drilled crankshaft (believed to be coming into production).

10. We are using oil cooler pipes supplied by Oil Feed Engineering and not Smiths. (The Smith ones collapsed when bent.)

11. Straight cut close ratio gears.

12. The rear suspension has orange struts and 30 lb. helper springs, part No. 21A 1566, together with red and double red displacer units (these have been listed on the homologation form as heavy duty export suspension). The piston stems front and rear have been modified by .165".

BMC Competitions Department Secrets ...

BMC COMPETITIONS COMMITTEE

Minutes of the Meeting held at Longbridge on 11th November, 1966

Present: Mr. H.J. Suffield
Mr. A.A. Issigonis
Mr. S. Turner

1. **1967 Rallying**

   i) It was decided to continue rallying in 1967, but on a reduced scale (20% less than in 1966). During the season an effort should be made to win classes with the 1800 range, while still running the 1275s for outright win attempts. As well as attempting to boost sales, a shift of emphasis to the 1800s would obviate saturation with advertising of the "Mini Wins Again" variety.

   ii) A programme as shown in Addendum A was agreed. This shows a reduction of effort in Eastern Bloc countries; the only new event is the Corsican which is of increasing importance in French markets. Innocenti will be consulted before the Italian Rally in case it is possible to run cars with their badge.

   iii) A certain amount of freedom will be allowed in the programme agreed in ii) in case a shift of emphasis becomes necessary either because of market conditions or driver championships. As an example, it was agreed that it would be a good psychological move to find an appropriate event in Japan and beat them on their home ground to counteract the heavy pro-Japanese publicity currently running.

   iv) The World Rally Championship was discussed but as it includes events like the Safari for which we do not enter it was decided not to make any effort in this competition.

   v) It was decided not to enter the Safari Rally. If one of our team drivers wins a free trip to Africa as a prize on another event then a car will be prepared for them and sold afterwards to Benbros.

   vi) It was decided not to enter the Shell 4000 (Canada).

   vii) Cars for the Police Rally were discussed and in view of the present unsatisfactory arrangement for allocating cars it was decided that Fleet Sales should have a say in the placing of any cars loaned in future.

2. **1967 Racing**

   i) Mr. Issigonis stated that as far as he knew, Jaguar have no plans for a return to racing. It was agreed that if an event arose for which a Jaguar was the only suitable model in the joint range, then the Competition Manager would raise the question at a higher level.

   ii) It was agreed that the Donald Healey Motor Co. should have the same budget for 1967 as in 1966, i.e., £15,000.

Lester Suffield had joined the Competitions Committee by the time I attended for the last time in 1966. John Thornley was absent due to illness. Point 1(iii) reflects the growing concern over the threat from Japan while (vii) shows that the blasted Police Rally was an ongoing item. Point 1(iv) indicates that the World Rally Championship was not considered important then.

1961 to 1967: THE MIDDLE YEARS by Stuart Turner

Planning a programme became more difficult as some of the great events, like the Alpine and Liège, dropped off the calendar.

iii) An entry of two MGs will be made in the Florida 12-hours, together with one Mini if there is a suitable sedan race. This will probably be backed by a Donald Healey Motor Co. entry.

iv) Because of prevailing speed differentials, it was decided not to enter any MGs at Le Mans in 1967. However it was decided to consider a press hospitality test.

v) As the oldest motor race, the Targa Florio attracts reasonable publicity and it was decided to enter one or two MGs in 1967 (depending on the regulations), probably backed by a Healey entry.

vi) It was decided to enter one or two cars in the "Marathon de la Route" provided it is possible under the regulations to repeat our 1966 win. It was agreed that long distance events like the Marathon and the Targa are the best competition show-cases for the sports car range.

vii) <u>Saloon Car Racing</u>

    a) No entries will be made in the 1967 European Saloon Car Championship.

    b) It was decided that John Cooper should once again enter cars in the British Saloon Car Championship, in association with Downtons and Engines Branch. However, the situation will be reviewed after the first few races to see if the new cylinder head has made the 1275 any more competitive.

3. <u>Cars for 1967</u>

i) It was pointed out that the 1275 was being overtaken by the opposition but our 1967 attack will have to rest with this, backed up by the MGC when announced. It was pointed out that the maximum co-operation will be needed from all departments in order to develop the "C" to rally-winning trim in the shortest possible time.

ii) In an attempt to avoid Morris dealer protests when an Austin 1275 wins, and vice versa, Mr. Issigonis agreed to ask Mr. Dick Burzi to investigate standardising Austin and Morris versions of the 1275, possibly by simply showing "Mini Cooper 'S'" fore and aft with a common radiator grille and steering wheel badge. This would also assist future homologation of the car.

iii) The possibility of installing a Daimler or Climax engine in an MGC for a limited 50-off run as a prestige sports car was considered. It is understood that the $2\frac{1}{2}$ litre Climax engine will fit in the MGC. Mr. Issigonis agreed to progress the matter further. It was pointed out that the reduced 1967 rally programme would mean that such a car could be built by Competitions and/or Special Tuning at Abingdon.

BMC Competitions Department Secrets ...

Point 5 (i) and (ii) show just how sensitive the company could be at times.

- 3 -

4. **Trade Contracts**

   a) It was agreed that BMC competition cars must continue to run on Dunlop tyres. Mr. Issigonis said that if any shortcomings were found in their products or service, then he would take things up at the highest level.

   b) It was agreed that safety belts were a matter of driver preference, although it was pointed out that in any case the rally team would probably change from Irving to Britax for 1967.

   c) After consideration of proposals from Castrol and Shell for our competition work in 1967 it was decided to remain with Castrol, whose advertising proposals were far more extensive.

5. **Other Points**

   i) It was decided that the Special Tuning Department should not advertise in the technical press. Mr. Suffield stated that he was anxious to avoid any suggestion of direct retail selling by BMC. During a discussion of tuning work it was stated that the "warm" work would be given to Downtons (the necessary parts being stocked by BMC Service) while the "hot" tuning, invalidating warranties, would be done by Special Tuning.

   ii) A request from Marcos Cars for the loan of two rally tuned 1275 engines for Le Mans 1967 was considered. The request was granted although it was to be made clear that this was a one-off loan which in no way implied any tie-up between BMC and Marcos.

   iii) It was noted that Vitafoam are to continue their association with BMC by campaigning our cars next season.

   iv) A record attempt with an 1800 was agreed. This would be a joint venture between Competitions, Downtons and Castrol. Downtons would be responsible for the preparation of the engine unit, Competitions for the preparation of the car and the organisation, and Castrol for technical (and financial) assistance.

   v) The lavish Ford bonus scheme (covering isolated rallies) was discussed but it was decided to maintain our present all-embracing scheme.

   vi) A contribution of £5000 to the competition expenses of BMC Canada was agreed.

   vii) It was decided that no contribution be made to BMC/Hambro competition expenses in 1967.

1961 to 1967: THE MIDDLE YEARS by Stuart Turner

This page from the team instructions for the 1967 Monte Carlo Rally, on which we were hoping to avenge the disqualification the previous year, highlights yet again the importance placed on accurate ice notes.

MONTE 1967   4.

TEAMS have been entered as follows:

A	B
144 Makinen	14 Jones
177 Aaltonen	32 Fall
205 Hopkirk	178 Lampinen

BAGGAGE

Any cases delivered to Comps by Sunday 8th January will be taken to the Helder by our van although Lisbon, Athens and Dover service crews should be able to cope with luggage for Makinen/Easter, Hopkirk/Crellin and Fall/Joss Aaltonen/Liddon and Lampinen/Wood may already have cases in Monte.

ICE NOTES

Each co-driver must leave one set of pace notes for each test at the Garage Auber. These notes will be handed out at or near the start of each test with these markings:

    Underlined in pencil = road <u>wet</u> when ice notes made (i.e., if, say, on Ventoux the first corner with a pencil line you come to is frozen it is likely that all the others will be too).

    Broken underlining in red = patchy snow or ice

    Underlined in red = snow or ice.

Don't forget to carry a second set of pace notes with you in case the ice note system breaks down.

N.B. If possible leave your Granier notes at Abingdon for T. Ambrose to take out to Geneva (otherwise will be delivered to him by R. Brown/S. Bradford).

PHONE NUMBERS

    Athens hotel: 237.611
    Lisbon hotel: 735121
    Dover hotel: Dover 1184
    Monte hotel: 30.63.07
    N. Higgins: Sutton Courtenay 295
    N. Challis: Didcot 2710
    Garage Auber: Nice 88.75.20
    Esso Service Buckel: Cap d'Ail 82.23.80
    Kennings: Lyon (78) 49-90-50 (ask for Mr. Plottier)
    "L'Escapade": Bedoin 21.

FLYING DOCTOR

If a car has trouble early in the rally drivers or mex should phone England as soon as possible with exact details of parts needed. If possible a mechanic will fly further up the route to intercept the rally (Messrs. Higgins and Challis to liaise and arrange).

GENERAL POINTS

(<u>drivers</u> and mex must read these)

1. ALL mechanics must be at meetings at the Helder at:

    07.00 on Tuesday, 17th January

    and

    10.00 on Thursday, 19th January

5.

2. Service crews must always have one or two spare bags of petrol in case there is a lot of work to be done and a car has no time to go to pumps.

3. Mex must study the fuel arrangements carefully. Watch the fire risk with the inevitable spectators. Have FIRE EXTINGUISHERS near at hand.

4. If T. Fall stays at the George Hotel, Dorchester, on his way to Dover will he please refrain from smothering his steaks in HP Sauce - we have had complaints from the chef.

5. Works cars take <u>absolute</u> priority at service points but help others when time. Give particular attention to number 66 (Koob) who is BMC sponsored.

6. Works drivers who drop out will be expected to lend a hand later in the event.

7. 16 strokes on our hand pumps = 1 gallon.

8. If acquits are shown going IN to a country then they MUST be cleared going OUT.

9. Mini roof racks must be taken off rally cars on arrival in Monte.

10. Cars starting the rally with numerous petrol bags on board must either take them to Monte or give them to service cars; they form a vital part of later fuel plans.

11. Fluid will be carried in barges and service cars to protect against carbs. icing up.

12. Service crews must remember that the rally does not really start until Monte; save any late night revelry until the Mountain Circuit is over.

13. IT IS THE CO-DRIVERS' RESPONSIBILITY TO SAY HOW LONG CAN BE SPARED AT A SERVICE POINT.

14. Works service cars will have the usual octagon signs. Agents en route have been asked to display 'BMC'. Crews should stop at these points if time to encourage them to help us again.

15. Don't weight your rally car down with junk. All service cars will eventually get to Monte so swimming togs and surplus sweeties can safely be given to them.

16. When service crews are given ice notes to hand out it is vital that these are given to the right cars. Co-drivers must put their rally number on their notes.

17. Cars will have a lot of time in hand at many controls on the run to Monte; service cars should scout out local hotels in case crews have time for a sleep or bath.

18. Consult co-drivers in Monte over the best place to service if doubt over any places on the Chambery leg and Mountain Circuit.

19. The eight tyres allowed for the Chambery leg will be fitted in a 20 minute period soon after cars arrive in Monte from 11.43 on Monday 16th January. As we will have more tyres than wheels some efficient tyre fitting may be needed.

The eight tyres for the Mountain Circuit will be fitted to the best 60 cars sometime during the afternoon of Thursday 19th January - service cars needed for this will be notified at 10.00.

20. The regs say "All refuelling and any assistance on the public highway are prohibited on all itineraries between the arrival and departure points in Monaco and the towns of Menton and La Turbie.

However/

A further page from the '67 Monte instructions. Point 4 Tony Fall was a very popular member of the team and, along with Mike Wood, cheerfully gave as good as he got when ribbed about being "a northern lad". This note was just part of the process. Point 15 Reducing weight has always seemed to me to be the quickest and cheapest way to improve the power-to-weight ratio. Point 19 The restriction on tyres caused much discussion and, maybe unfairly, was seen by some as a 'stop the Minis' scheme. In fact, the event ran fairly smoothly.

BMC Competitions Department Secrets ...

Point 29 This referred to an experiment the Council was doing to record the heart rates of various sportsmen when at full stretch.

Point 32 I don't know whose medical evidence I'd read but it seemed to be a sensible point to include.

6.

However the club confirm that, as last year, service can be done in garages <u>off the public highway</u>. When cars first arrive in Monte and after the Chambery leg, service will therefore be at Esso Service Buckel, Moyenne Corniche, Cap d'Ail, tel: Cap d'Ail 82.23.80 (as used last year).

21. Although once the rally gets to Monte we are restricted in the number of tyres used, <u>wheels and inner tubes</u> are free. All service cars must have spare wheels and tubes <u>and mex must practise tube changing</u>.

22. The regs say "It is prohibited for any competitor to park or stop on the highway or at the side of it at a distance of less than 100 metres from a time or passage control post or an arrival or starting point of the classification tests.

    MEX MUST WATCH THIS! As a general rule work before controls but in the later stages mex must be mobile enough to run through a control to work on the other side as well if necessary.

23. Where mex have rally cars put on their passports they must transfer them to the drivers before the rally starts.

24. Co-drivers will appreciate that many service points are emergency only.

25. Our cars will be closer together when the best 60 do the Mountain Circuit. An order of priority for work will be given to mex at the 10.00 meeting on 19th.

26. Mex will be given petrol money for the two legs from Monte at the meetings at the Helder.

27. Preventive maintenance will be vital. DON'T PASS THE BUCK to the next service point, no matter how cold it is.

28. If the organisers amend times for the Chambery leg and the Mountain Circuit these will be given out at mex meetings.

29. One service car may have to find space for a doctor from the Medical Research Council - this will be decided in Monte.

30. Additional wheels <u>and tyres</u> may be used during the run to Monte and all service cars must carry two pop-ins.

    After Monte the service cars must only carry spare wheels and tubes. To avoid any accusation of cheating service cars must NOT carry tyres after Monte.

31. Rally and service cars must have plenty of special wheel nuts.

32. According to medical evidence, it takes time for your eyes to re-adjust after being in bright light. At controls where there are press and TV cameras etc. it may help to wear sunglasses. It's worth looking a birkinshaw at a control if you are quicker on a subsequent test.

33. If there are no control addresses in these instructions (due to non-arrival) service crews going to start points should get details from the co-drivers or, failing this, consult the cops in control towns.

34. On the Chambery leg leave service points <u>immediately</u> the last works car has gone through, unless indicated otherwise elsewhere in these instructions.

    On Mountain Circuit most service crews see rally several times at same place but they must study the route so that they know from which direction to expect cars.

    Service space may be difficult so be in position in plenty of time.

7.

35. The armchair passengers' seat weights 41 lbs. A standard Mini seat with a cover (as used last year) weighs only 18 lbs. Five of these will be taken to Monte in the van to be fitted when you arrive.

36. There has been some difficulty in getting currency for such a large party. Therefore, in case there are investigations later, mex must note that expense accounts will be under particular scrutiny especially regarding hotels, petrol etc.

ADDITIONAL POINTS FOR SOME MEX.

S. Bradford/J. Smith/M. Legg/D. Pike/N. Hall/R. Vokins/D. Green/G. Wiffen.

The Abingdon van must take some tyres for ice note cars (depending on space and availability), 4 drums, 3 pumps, 3 full spares kits, 2 emergency kits and 10 service signs.

One full spares kit stays in van.

One full spares kit and two service signs go in French van at Nice for Hall to use.

One full spares kit and two service signs go in Castrol van at Nice for Vokins.

The two emergency kits stay in the Abingdon van as far as Riez. D. Green/G. Wiffen/D. Pike with A110 run to Riez in convoy with M. Legg/J. Smith in Abingdon van. (If there is a recce Mini left in running order this can be taken along as well).

Three mex in two cars will arrive at Riez from Kennings (Lyon) at 12.30 on 17th.

G. Wiffen with one Lyon mech, one emergency kit, two service signs and one Lyon car goes to Banon.

D. D. Pike with one Lyon mech, one emergency kit, five petrol bags and two service signs goes to Sault. Service there at junction of D164/N542. Cars will come <u>near</u> to this point an hour or so before they arrive along D164 and can nip along to you if in any trouble. D. Pike is interested in <u>second</u> arrival when you give them petrol.

D. Green with one Lyon mech and A110 and full kit goes to Bedoin.

<u>After</u> rally has gone through:

M. Legg/J. Smith go from Riez to Digne.

G. Wiffen and Lyon mech stay at Banon until D. Green arrives.

D. Green and Lyon mech go from Bedoin to Banon, D. Green/G. Wiffen then proceed to Monteferrat in A110 and two Lyon mex leave in Lyon car. (G. Wiffen's emergency kit will have to be stored in A110 from Banon).

D. Pike/Lyon mech go from Sault to Remollon to service. After rally has gone through Remollon they go to Gap where Pike gets lift to Monte with R. Vokins and Lyon mech. leaves with Kennings car. R. Vokins must stay at Gap until D. Pike arrives. D. Pike emergency kit goes in R. Vokins' van.

N.B. Mex working in French or Castrol vehicles must have two Minilite wheels with them!

R. Brown/M. Legg/D. Pike must arrange things in Monte before start so that one or two devote some time to fettling recce cars to be used by ice note crews.

D. Green/G. Wiffen Don't wait in Athens until rally starts but push ahead of it.

This gives just an inkling of how complicated life could be for mechanics on the Monte.

1961 to 1967: THE MIDDLE YEARS by Stuart Turner

MONTE 1967 - ADDITIONS AND ALTERATIONS TO INSTRUCTIONS   18.

REVISED ___ PLANS

5 works Minis.

Starts to Monte: 4 ½ pop-ins, 2 full pop-ins, 2 chisels and/or 2 knobs depending on availability.

Choice of tyres for Chambery leg:

8 plain SP3s, 8 plain SP44s, 6 ½ pop-ins, 4 ¾ pop-ins, 6 full pop-ins, 4 full knobs, 4 racers. (It may be possible to fit knobs to an ex recce car for drivers who have never used knobs to get a little practice) This selection will be <u>duplicated</u> for the Mountain Circuit.

Summary of tyres available once cars get to Monte:

	TOTAL	Pop-ins ½	Pop-ins ¾	Pop-ins Full	SP3	SP 44	Racers	Full Knobs
To Monte by Dunlops for Chambery leg	180	30	20	30	40	40	20	
To Monte by Dunlops for Mountain Circuit	180	30	20	30	40	40	20	
(Specials) to Monte by Dunlops for emergency studding (Finn mex taking 5000 studs to Monte).	20					20		
Totals taken by Dunlops	380	60	40	60	80	100	40	-
By air from Helsinki to Nice: (Chambery	20							20
(M. Circuit	20							20
TOTALS	420	60	40	60	80	100	40	40

OTHER POINTS

1.) Plain SP44s will be split 50% normal/50% TT.

2.) Dunlops' fitters in Monte are staying at Hotel Russi, B. Carrothers at the Metropole.

3. Marks made on the tyres by the organisations, quote, "will have to be found right in front of the valve. Should the competitor be lead to remove one of his tyres, he will have to take care that the mark will be found at the same place.

   In view to avoid the competitor a loss of time during the controls, it is essential that the spare tyres will be stored in the car or in the boot in such a way that the identification marks will be easily apparent."

   This means that spares on the back seat must be stored outside up.

4. "Cars will be considered as being in closed parks as soon as they arrive at the Control Quai Albert Ier. Beside the changing of tyres, competitors will not be allowed to make any refuelling nor any repairs under pain of being <u>excluded from the Rally</u>".

5. "Special" tyres for BMC will have a <u>yellow</u> band running from bead to bead; if the tyres are originally fitted with <u>this band near to the valve</u> it will help mex to ensure that the organisers identifying marks remain in the right place if refitting tyres after a puncture or wheel change.

6. Some tyres may have a mixture of studs. Therefore when a tyre has a <u>red colour code</u> on one wall it is to be fitted with this to the <u>outside</u>.

7. Plenty of special wheel nuts must be carried in rally cars and barges.

8. ... small clear plastic bottle contains enough anti-icing fluid to go in ... gallons of petrol.

9. The Castrol contingent are staying at the Alessandria.

10. Will ice note crews please check the navigation notes for the Mountain Circuit (which are largely last years').

11. There is no need for S. Bradford/J. Smith to take studded tyres to Nice for ice note cars (Dunlops in Nice should have a supply at the Auber).

<u>Wheels</u> needed:
- 5 cars from start points.................50
- On 6 service cars as spares.............12
- In Dunlop van to Monte for Chambery leg......40
- In Dunlop van to Monte for Mountain Circuit..40
- In Dunlop van to Monte as extra spares.......10

Total 152

Although there were limits on the number of tyres allowed on the '67 Monte, the tyre plan still looked pretty complicated. The Dunlop fitters were always a huge support, and were, in effect, full members of the team.

BMC Competitions Department Secrets ...

(Swedish)
Härmed intygas att innehavaren af detta kort reser på den europeiska kontinenten på uppdrag av The British Motor Corporation och The M.G. Car Co. och att denna person är berättigad att köra av oss ägda bilar samt på våra vägnar underteckna fordons— och resedokument.

(Danish)
Herved attesteres at indehaveren af kortet er på rejse i Europa på 'The British Motor Corporation' og 'M.G. Car Co.' 's vegne og er berettiget til at køre biler, som tilhører os, og til at underskrive automobil- og rejsedokumenter på vore vegne.

(Greek)
Βεβαιούται, ότι ὁ κάτοχος τοῦ παρόντος δελτίου ταξιδεύει εἰς Εὐρώπην διὰ λογαριασμόν τῆς British Motor Corporation καὶ τῆς M. G. Car Company καὶ δικαιοῦται νὰ ὁδηγῇ αὐτοκίνητα τῆς Ἑταιρείας μας καὶ νὰ ὑπογράφῃ ταξιδιωτικὰ κλπ. ἔγγραφα διὰ λογαριασμόν μας.

(Bulgarian)
Удостоверяваме с настоящето, че носителя на тази карта пътува из Европа от името на British Motor Corporation (Бритиш Мотор Корпорейшън) и на M. G. Car Co. (M. Г. Кар Компани).
Той има правото да кара автомобилните коли наша собственост и да подписва от наше име автомобилни и пътни документи.

(Serbo-Croat)
Ovime se poturdjuje da nosioc ove legitimacije putuje u Evropu u ime British Motor Corporation i M.G. Car Co. te da je ovlasten da vozi kola koja su nase vlasnistvo i kao tako ovlasten moze da potpisuje putne naloge i dokumente koji se odnose na automobile u nase ime.

BRITISH MOTOR CORPORATION

COMPETITIONS DEPARTMENT

The M.G. Car Co. Ltd., Abingdon, Berkshire

Telephone: Abingdon 251
Telegrams: EMGEE, Abingdon

Form No. .... 8 ....

Valid until .... 31st. December 1967 ....

Name of holder .... S. Turner ....

Signature of holder

This is to certify that the holder of this card is travelling on the Continent of Europe on behalf of The British Motor Corporation and the M.G. Car Co., Ltd., and is entitled to drive cars owned by us and to sign vehicle and travel documents on our behalf.

For and on behalf of The British Motor Corporation and The M.G. Car Co. Ltd.

Director & General Manager

Competitions Manager

(French)
Nous certifions par la présente que le détenteur de cette carte voyage sur le continent d'Europe au nom de la British Motor Corporation et de la M.G. Car Co. et est autorisé à conduire des voitures nous appartenant et à signer en notre nom les papiers du véhicule et les documents de voyage.

(German)
Hiermit wird bescheinigt, dass der Inhaber dieser Karte im Auftrage der British Motor Corporation und der M.G. Car Co. auf dem europäischen Festland reist und berechtigt ist, in unserem Besitz befindliche Wagen zu fahren und Fahrzeugpapiere und Reisedokumente in unserem Namen zu unterzeichnen.

(Dutch)
Wij verklaren hierbij dat de houder van de kaart op het vasteland van Europa reist namens de British Motor Corporation en de M.G. Car Co., en dat hij het recht heeft om auto's te besturen in eigendom bij ons en om voertuig— en reisdokumenten namens ons te tekenen.

(Italian)
Certifichiamo con la presente che il latore della cartolina viaggia sul continente Europeo per conto della British Motor Corporation e della M.G. Car Company ed è autorizzato a guidare le automobili a noi appartenenti ed a firmare per conto nostro i documenti relativi ai veicoli ed al viaggio.

This was produced to try and help us through customs points, which could sometimes be difficult. We forget now that, back then, the documents needed for travel with cars – and especially spares – were complicated. It was perhaps not surprising that we sometimes found it easier to change chassis plates and registration numbers on the cars than to prepare fresh documentation. Doing this once left us with a Mini on a rally with a Morris badge on one end and an Austin on the other, which neither customs, police or scrutineers noticed! These permutations, plus the frequency with which cars were re-shelled, have left me slightly jaundiced about claims that "this is the actual car in which X won the Y rally". I always have a pinch of salt handy when I hear this ...

1961 to 1967: THE MIDDLE YEARS by Stuart Turner

A busy Competitions Department in 1962 with Mini-Cooper, Sprite, MGA, big Healey, A40 and Midget being prepared for the Monte Carlo Rally.

Peter Riley, who helped the team net a crop of class wins on the 1962 Monte Carlo Rally, is seen here leaving the East Grinstead time control.

Stuart Turner arrived at Abingdon with the Mini-Cooper already showing its potential, and the big Austin-Healey fully developed as a rally winner.

1961 to 1967: THE MIDDLE YEARS by Stuart Turner

BMC Competitions Department Secrets ...

The Reverend Rupert Jones in dog collar tackles the Monaco Grand Prix circuit, with one of the last 850 Mini entries, at the end of the 1962 Monte Carlo Rally in which he finished 3rd in class.

Don Morley on his way to a class win on the 1962 Monte Carlo Rally with one of the final pairs of MGAs built for rallying, using the Coupé with knock-off disc wheels and disc brakes all round.

1961 to 1967: THE MIDDLE YEARS by Stuart Turner

Testing at Silverstone for Sebring in 1962, where three MGA Coupés were entered for Jack Sears (left), Bob Oltoff, and John Whitmore. Jack Sears, paired with Andrew Hedges, finished 16th.

Paddy Hopkirk, keen to join the BMC team to get his hands on the Austin-Healey, had his first drive with the team on the 1962 Liège.

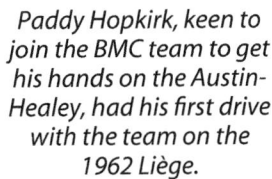

Breakthrough for the Mini – Pat Moss and Ann Wisdom survived this spot of plug trouble to exploit the handicap to win the 1962 Tulip Rally, the Mini-Cooper's first international victory.

1961 to 1967: THE MIDDLE YEARS by Stuart Turner

Erik Carlsson takes part in a secret test session to try out the Mini-Cooper. Stuart Turner tried, without success, to persuade him to leave Saab to join BMC.

Stuart Turner ordered new recruit Timo Makinen to drive "without any fireworks" on his first event with BMC, the 1962 RAC Rally. He finished 7th, winning the class: the start of a legendary career with the team.

1961 to 1967: THE MIDDLE YEARS by Stuart Turner

Class winners Logan Morrison and Brian Culcheth, at the Glasgow start of the 1963 Monte Carlo Rally.

Paddy Hopkirk swings round the harbour test at Monaco in 1963 to take 6th overall on his first Monte with the full Mini team; Rauno Aaltonen finished third.

Scrabbling for traction, the big Healey of Timo Makinen and Christabel Carlisle descends the Turini on the 1963 Monte Carlo Rally.

1961 to 1967: THE MIDDLE YEARS by Stuart Turner

Timo Makinen, with steam pouring out of the bottom radiator hose, turns into Casino Square on the 1963 Monte Carlo Rally with a works Ford Falcon hard on his heels. He won the GT category, finishing 13th overall.

BMC Competitions Department Secrets ...

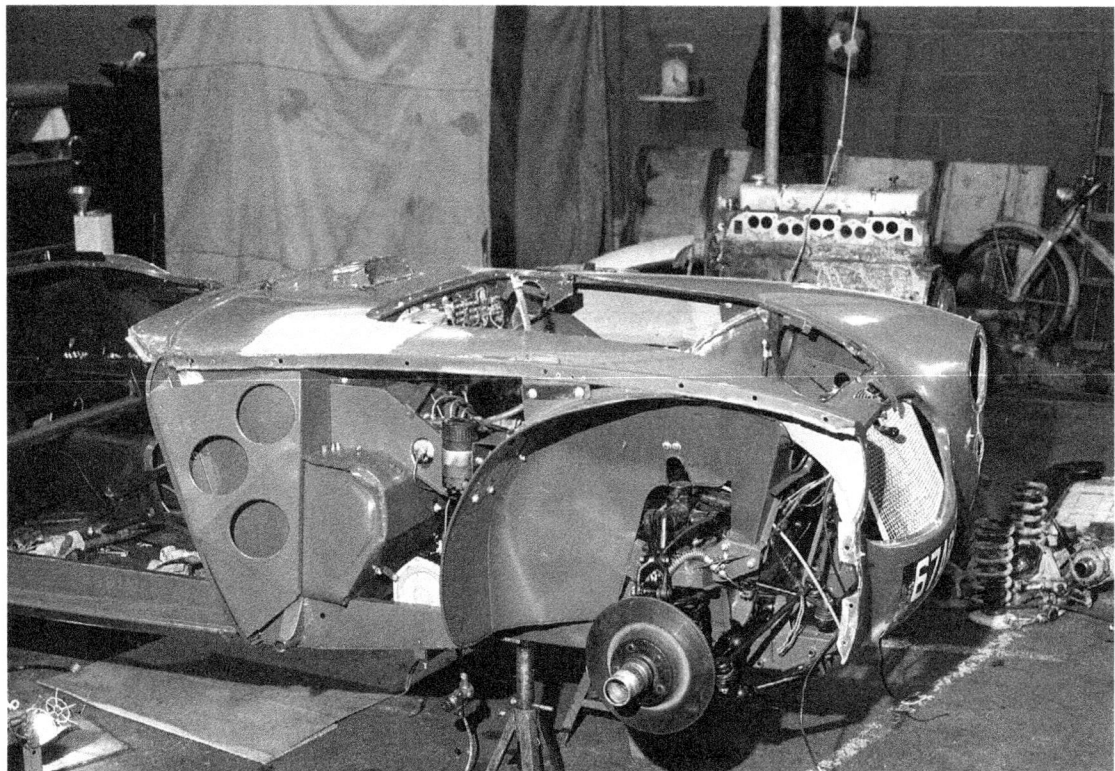

Works big Healey 67 ARX undergoing a ground-up rebuild in 1963.

Glum looks from Paddy Hopkirk, left, as the Minis receive attention in France on the 1964 Monte Carlo Rally.

1961 to 1967: THE MIDDLE YEARS by Stuart Turner

Timo Makinen, trying very hard as always on the final round-the-houses Monaco sprint in 1964, finishing 4th; he would win the following year.

Mini wins the Monte! Paddy Hopkirk and Henry Liddon heading for victory in 1964, and the first of a run of Mini Monte wins for the Abingdon team.

The Morley brothers scored a convincing outright win in the GT category of the 1964 Monte Carlo Rally, which was to stand as the best rallying result for the MGB.

1961 to 1967: THE MIDDLE YEARS by Stuart Turner

On stage at Sunday Night at the London Palladium, where millions of TV viewers saw Paddy Hopkirk, Henry Liddon and the 1964 Monte winning Mini-Cooper.

Tony Fall on a test-it-to-destruction session in Wales.

1961 to 1967: THE MIDDLE YEARS by Stuart Turner

Timo Makinen and Don Barrow on the 1964 Liège – they set such a furious pace over roads like this that they shredded their tyres.

BMC Competitions Department Secrets ...

Rauno Aaltonen and Tony Ambrose deliver the big Healey's final international outright victory on the last ever Liège of 1964.

Pauline Mayman and Val Domleo swing round Porlock hairpin on the 1964 RAC Rally in this Abingdon MGB – they retired with clutch problems.

1961 to 1967: THE MIDDLE YEARS by Stuart Turner

The Morley brothers take Wales by storm on the 1964 RAC Rally.

A pair of Austin 1800s were tried on the 1965 Monte Carlo Rally, John Sprinzel, Courtney Edwards and Tommy Wisdom finishing 31st after brake problems on the final section.

1961 to 1967: THE MIDDLE YEARS by Stuart Turner

On the rack: gas bottles, hydrolastic pump, rubber fuel bags, quick lift jack and Mini spare wheel (with two more wheels mounted on the boot lid), all held down with rubber bungee-bands on the roof of the Vanden Plas Princess R service car on the 1964 RAC Rally.

The Morley brothers receiving a tyre change on their way to finishing 8th on the 1965 Tulip Rally. Peter Browning, on the right with camera and clipboard, was acting as Competitions Press Officer.

The Morleys 'yumping' over the famous Carron Valley Bridge on the 1965 RAC Rally.

Rauno Aaltonen's winning Mini-Cooper stops for fresh SP44s on the 1965 RAC Rally.

1961 to 1967: THE MIDDLE YEARS by Stuart Turner

Timo Makinen with Paul Easter receive attention during their struggle to win the 1965 RAC Rally: they chalked up no fewer than 32 fastest stage times.

Battered but unbowed – Makinen's big Healey showing the scars of having been nudged into a snow bank in Pickering Forest on the 1965 RAC Rally.

1961 to 1967: THE MIDDLE YEARS by Stuart Turner

Rauno Aaltonen and Tony Ambrose, with ice packed in the wheels, take the lead on the 1965 RAC Rally to beat off a determined challenge from Timo Makinen. Rauno clinched the European Rally Championship with this victory.

The Abingdon Men. From left to right, top row: Den Green, Doug Watts, Dudley Pike, Brian Owen, Roy Brown, storeman Mike Partridge, Johnny Organ, Brian Moylan, Robin Vokins, Nobby Hall, Bill Price, Tommy Wellmam (white coat); front: Mick Hogan, Johnny Evans, Bob Whittington, Gerald Wiffen and Stan Bradford.

1961 to 1967: THE MIDDLE YEARS by Stuart Turner

Stuart Turner with Castrol's Ray Simpson (left), and Jimmy Hill, plus MG boss John Thornley.

Stan Chalmers, assistant to John Smith from Lucas, working at Abingdon. The intricate wiring looms made for the Minis and Austin-Healeys were works of art.

1966 Monte – 'Winners' Timo Makinen and Paul Easter.

1961 to 1967: THE MIDDLE YEARS by Stuart Turner

1966 Monte – Sheet ice and no studs for 'runners-up' Rauno Aaltonen and Tony Ambrose.

BMC Competitions Department Secrets ...

DISQUALIFIED!

1966 Monte – Paddy Hopkirk and Henry Liddon, with luggage straps holding a spotlight in place, on their way to 'third' place.

1961 to 1967: THE MIDDLE YEARS by Stuart Turner

Rauno Aaltonen and Henry Liddon on the 1966 RAC Rally, beaten into 4th place by guest Mini driver Harry Kallstrom, who finished 2nd overall.

BMC Competitions Department Secrets ...

Tony Fall and Mike Wood on the 1966 Alpine Rally. Three Minis retired, including this one, but Rauno Aaltonen took 3rd overall.

The 'office' of a works Mini-Cooper.

1961 to 1967: THE MIDDLE YEARS by Stuart Turner

The retirement lunch for Don and Erle Morley in 1966 in Abingdon's boardroom (with portrait of MG founder Cecil Kimber behind). Left to right: Jack Gardner (Personnel Manager), Doug Gardner (Works Engineer), Les Lambourne (Material Controller), Stuart Turner (Competitions Manager), Don Morley, Charlie Martin (Progress Manager), Erle Morley, Doug Watts (Competitions Foreman), Norman Higgins (Financial Controller), John Thornley (MG Director and General Manager).

Last event for Stuart Turner; the 1967 Monte Carlo Rally where he talks tyres with Timo Makinen and Dunlop personnel.

1967-1970

THE END OF THE LINE

Peter Browning

Preface

My only reservation about contributing to this book was that under the fraught and unhappy circumstances of leaving Abingdon when it was closed down by British Leyland in 1970, I was not able to retrieve any of the Competitions Department files or significant archive documents. In fact, the British Leyland policy instruction regarding closure of the Department included the strict edict that all of the Competitions files, records, car build sheets and photographic archive should actually be destroyed.

I was incensed by this but did manage to rescue the bound volumes of the car build sheets (which went back many years through Stuart's and Marcus' eras), and I also smuggled out of the factory the photo archives. I am pleased to say that, subsequently, I have been able to ensure that the invaluable build sheets have been copied and passed on to the owners of ex-works cars (and friends within the Mini-Cooper Register, MG Car Club and Austin-Healey Club). The photo collection continues to be used to illustrate books and articles.

My contribution, therefore, comprises personal comments and stories on a mixture of subjects which, with the passing of time, I hope are relevant and interesting.

The route to Abingdon

It was probably inevitable that motorsport would dominate my life as my father raced at Brooklands, was a founder member of the Veteran Car Club, a former Vice President of the Vintage Sports Car Club, and later a senior RAC Scrutineer and BRDC Member.

I joined my local Harrow Car Club in north London in 1955 with my first car, a Morris Minor, and found myself competing against such luminaries as Pat Moss and John Sprinzel who were keen members. One of my closest buddies at the time was Brian Culcheth who joined me in the team at Abingdon in later years. With the HCC we competed in every form of motorsport: rallies, autocross, driving tests and hillclimbs, and even raced as members of the Eight Clubs at Silverstone.

However, I soon discovered that I was more suited to organising events than competing in them, and, as a result of a chance meeting with Wilson McComb, formerly with *Autosport,* who had just joined MG to edit *Safety Fast* magazine, I received an invitation from John Thornley (MG General Manager) to come to Abingdon and set up the Austin-Healey Club alongside the MG Car Club.

I was soon co-opted to join the *Safety Fast* magazine team and, as the offices were opposite the hallowed Competitions Department, I obviously took more than a passing interest in the comings and goings of cars and drivers.

Before I came to Abingdon I had been an RAC timekeeper, the youngest, I am told, to gain a full international grading, and Stuart Turner (totally involved with the rallying side) asked me to help out with the running of the MG racing entries. Through my Austin-Healey Club connections I also got to

1967 to 1970: THE END OF THE LINE by Peter Browning

work with Geoff Healey with the works Healey entries, and went along to Le Mans, Sebring, the Targa Florio, and the Nürburgring with the works teams.

My introduction to the works rally team came when I later went on events as Competitions Press Officer. In these useful years of apprenticeship I had got to know the drivers, mechanics and supporting trade people pretty well. Nevertheless, I was not prepared when, at the end of 1966, John Thornley called me into his office and told me that Stuart was leaving and he wanted me to take over. I remember saying that I could not possibly do the job (probably subsequently endorsed by many members of the team!) but John was insistent, so that was that.

MGB MARATHON

One of my earlier and most rewarding outings with the works MGs, before I took over from Stuart, was on the 1966 84 Hour Marathon at the Nürburgring.

When the regulations for this event arrived at Abingdon it immediately appealed to me as a personal challenge as pit manager, being basically a mammoth regularity race around the full 17.5 mile circuit. Each car was given a bogey lap time according to its number of seats and engine size. If you failed to maintain your speed you were docked race distance penalties, but the margins were tight and serious penalties were incurred for spending too long on allocated pit stop times.

With much work on the slide rule we reckoned that a sensibly driven MGB would do well, on the basis that the car should be totally reliable and just about quick enough to keep up the pace. Stuart agreed to the preparation of a pair of cars, released a handful of mechanics, and gave us a modest budget for our four drivers – Andrew Hedges/Julien Vernaeve and Roger Enever/Alec Poole.

The drivers did an illegal recce the night before the start to familiarise themselves with the circuit, and with our pits converted with blow-up tents for the on-duty mechanics and Moulton bikes for the drivers to get to their hotel, the race got under way.

The opposition was impressive with everything from works Porsches and Alan Mann's hot Cortinas, to Equipe National Belge GTB Ferraris – all with serious professional driving talent.

The MGs made a nightmare start. Since the team had recced the circuit one of the corners had been resurfaced and left covered with loose chippings. Hedges was the first to go off into a field though, thankfully, kept going to find a suitable gap in the hedge to jump back onto the track. Poole almost did the same thing, disappearing down a ditch, but again kept going and rejoined the circuit. On lap one the two MGs came through last, limped into the pits needing urgent repairs, the most serious being the Hedges car which had a holed fuel tank and most of the lights knocked akimbo. Den Green and the boys worked miracles and both cars rejoined the race, albeit in a humiliating last place.

The story of how the two MGs fought their way through the field to be running 1st and 2nd overall as the 84 hours drew to a close has been told many times, but was really down to two factors: the utter reliability of the cars, and the fact that our strategy was for the drivers to race for 10 laps (2.5 hours, 175 miles). Although this meant that they were pretty tired when they handed over, they then had a reasonable rest period. Most of the rival teams ran shorter sessions which meant that the less experienced drivers certainly could not keep up the pace toward the end of the event.

Although – sadly – the Enever/Poole car dropped out in the closing stages after a half shaft broke when pulling away from a refuelling stop, the Hedges/Vernaeve MGB cruised to a comfortable three lap victory over the Jacky Ickx Cortina, covering 5600 trouble-free racing miles.

When I phoned Stuart to tell him that we had won, he dryly commented that he would have expected us to win – the class. When I told him we had won outright he could not believe it!

MONTE DEBUT

My first event with the team was the 1967 Monte when I slid in alongside Stuart on what was his last event. This could not have been a more technically challenging and complicated introduction to the rallying team! I remember sitting in on one of Stuart's planning meetings when we went through the Dunlop tyre plans, and I have to admit that I was totally at sea!

This was the year that the Monte organisers, in their usual annual endeavour to change the rules to prevent all but the French winning, introduced the option of the tyre handicap. Essentially, if you had use of unlimited tyres a 12 per cent handicap was applied, otherwise the restriction was 8 tyres for the main competitive sections. We elected to go for the 8 tyres.

I remember an awful moment after the tyre planning meeting when Stuart gave me his handwritten master plan. I put it in the copying machine which had not warmed up properly, pressed the button and it shredded the original sheet to ribbons! Having sat through the meeting and given the impression that I had understood everything, I now had to try and reconstruct the vital document from memory!

I recall that I spent the whole of that Monte in a bit of a daze trying to get to grips with the servicing schedules, the ice note crews, the tyre schedules, and the thousand-and-one other aspects of the behind-the-scenes organisation. But it was a most satisfactory result, vindicating the much publicised Monte Mini disqualification of 1966 and bringing Stuart a Monte win for each of his stars – Paddy Hopkirk, Timo Makinen, and now Rauno Aaltonen.

The mechanics

I had not been long in the hot seat before I came to appreciate the quality of the Abingdon mechanics. Looking back, the amazing thing was that very few of them came into the Department with specific competitions experience. Hand-picked from various other departments, many joined as apprentices with particular aptitude and enthusiasm – some started as young tea boys. They learnt their trade by working alongside the more experienced men in the shop and in the field.

Unlike today's World Rally Championship teams, which have an army of highly trained specialists to handle each technical aspect of the cars, the BMC mechanics did everything themselves; building up the cars from trimmed bodyshells, engines, gearbox, suspension, brakes, chassis mods – the lot. And they used to run-in the cars themselves and, of course, go on the event to look after 'their' car.

The only area that they did not cover was electrics which was handled by resident Lucas technician John Smith, who wired all the cars from scratch. Interestingly, in proving the authenticity of ex-works cars today, it has often been the work of John Smith (and his assistant Stan Chalmers) which has proved vital. The unique way in which cable runs were made, the use of non-standard looms and special connectors, etc., have often provided the all-important provenance of an Abingdon-built car.

Build sheet

The works Minis were generally built from trimmed bodyshells which came as a convenient, readily available 'part'. Works MGBs and big Healeys were usually built up from cars taken off the assembly lines.

For each car an individual build sheet was prepared which detailed the specification of every single item from carburettor jet sizes to the co-driver's personal preference for door pocket leg padding. The build sheets ran into a dozen foolscap pages and when the car was complete they were filed in large leatherbound volumes.

After every event a very detailed questionnaire had to be filled in by both crew members, covering every aspect of the car's performance on the event. These were copied (uncensored) and circulated to appropriate heads of department, including supporting trade suppliers.

Success advertising

By the time I took over from Stuart the team was expected to win every time out – wherever the rally and whatever the opposition. There was a certain arrogance about it which I must say I found a bit scary!

This state of total optimism was typified by the regular pre-event briefing meetings which we used to have with the PR people and the advertising agency to agree the post event success advertising copy. Raymond Baxter was the PR Chief in my time – a splendid fellow who knew all about competitions. We knew each other from old Austin-Healey Club days when he was involved with founding the Sprite Club. Joining us at these meetings were the guys from Dorlands Advertising and we met in Raymond's office in Piccadilly. There, we would set out what we thought we could achieve on the forthcoming event: outright win, class or category awards, team prize, etc., and the advertising boys would write the copy there and then.

There was far more success advertising in those days than there is today, and the ads would

1967 to 1970: THE END OF THE LINE by Peter Browning

be scheduled alongside supporting trade ads from companies like Castrol and Dunlop. For the major events we would be talking about big ads in the nationals and motorsport magazines – big budget stuff. Nobody came away from the meeting with any thought that we might not win; but when that did happen Raymond and his men had always organised a standby ad for a Morris 1100 or something equally mundane!

Getting photos of the rally cars for the ads was always a problem because, inevitably, the cars would not be ready until the last moment, despite the pressure to make them available to the boys from the Cowley Photographic Department. Invariably the photos were taken either in the works car park or down a country road close by the factory. Rally plates and competition numbers might not always have been in place, which meant some crafty touching-up in the studio. It was difficult to make a car travelling down a leafy English lane at 30mph look as though it was flat out kicking up the dust in the wilds of Greece!

Talking of photos, we used to work very closely with BMC Photographic on the event to ensure that they knew where to go to get the best shots. Co-driver Henry Liddon was a keen photographer and I recall that he used to mark his road book notes on the recce with places where the photographers could get a good shot with the right background, ideal lighting and, most important, have an escape route so that they could quickly move on to the next location.

ANOTHER NEAR MONTE FIASCO

The 1968 Monte brought my first experience of being involved in an international technical confrontation with a rally organiser. Once again the Abingdon Minis were entered in force, and there was a determined effort from everyone to try and bring home another Monte victory. Everything went according to plan except for the weather for, apart from awful blizzards in Yugoslavia which had caused the Minis to run for the first time with chains, this was the first of a run of 'no-snow' years on the key competitive sections, which was to make our contest against Porsche – and Renault-Alpine in particular – almost impossible.

The results of the 1968 event were, perhaps, disappointing, but most people realised that in the circumstances we could not have achieved a better result. Rauno Aaltonen, Tony Fall and Paddy Hopkirk finished third, fourth and fifth overall behind the Porsches. They won the Team Prize and were placed 1-2-3 in the category.

Having said that everything went according to plan, that was not entirely so because this was the year of the carburettor controversy that very nearly caused as much of a rumpus as did those headlights in 1966.

For the first time we were using the twin split-Weber carburettors in Group II, developed and built at Abingdon from a prototype that Timo Makinen had seen in Finland. Basically, by cutting in half a pair of standard Weber carburettors, and fitting the two left-hand 'halves' on to the standard Group II inlet manifold, it was possible to achieve Group VI Weber-type performance in Group II (around 92bhp at 6500rpm). Cliff Humphries was responsible for this new development.

Having very carefully studied the Group II regulations, I was confident that the use of these carburettors was permissible. Nevertheless, I wrote to the FIA in Paris and to the Monte organisers many weeks before the event, enclosing details and photographs of our new carburettors. They thus had ample opportunity to raise any queries. To demonstrate that we had no intention of cheating, we passed details of the new engine specification to the press. Nobody said anything about it until we arrived in Monte.

After the Concentration Runs I was asked to attend a meeting of the Sporting Commission as, following initial technical inspection of the cars upon arrival in Monte, it had doubts about the eligibility of the carburettors, and wished to discuss my interpretation of the regulations covering this point. It was clear from the start that the Commission was doing this in a genuine attempt to safeguard BMC and the Rally from a repetition of the 1966 fiasco when, although aware at an early stage in the Rally of what was a possible infringement of the regulations, the Commission allowed the Mini crews to finish the event before disqualifying them. I was told there was no doubt that a protest would be forthcoming from other competitors if we continued using the new carburettors. I thanked the

Commission for the opportunity of this early discussion, and we all agreed that, for the good of the Monte and rallying in general, we should do everything possible to prevent a repetition of the 1966 debacle.

The English translation of the French regulations covering permitted carburettor alterations said: "The carburettors provided by the manufacturer may be replaced by others providing that the number be the same as that fitted by the manufacturer and that they can be mounted on the inlet manifold of the engine without using any intermediary device and by using the original attachment parts."

The Sporting Commission suggested that we had fitted an 'intermediary device' between the carburettors and the manifold. I replied that this was not so and explained that this was a prototype carburettor which, according to our interpretation of the regulations, began at the point of junction with the manifold and continued through the main body of the carburettor to the end of the inlet pipe.

Whilst the Sporting Commission was clearly divided over this point, the original French regulation was read and it was found that there was a discrepancy between the English and French texts. In the French text the interpretation of the final wording of the regulations read: "The carburettors must be mounted on the inlet manifold of the engine *without modification or deformation* and without using any intermediary device, and by using the original attachment parts." (The italicised words were omitted from the English text.)

Although concerned about the text discrepancy on a very significant point, we agreed that only the French text could be accepted as the official code. The Commission then felt that the carburettors were not eligible because we had modified them to make them fit the standard manifold. Again, I pointed out that we had not modified them because, although we had used basic Weber principles and some Weber design features and components, this was an entirely new prototype carburettor which we had designed and built in England. There could, therefore, be no question that we had modified it to make it fit the manifold; it was designed to fit in the first place. After one hour the meeting was adjourned for the Sporting Commission to make its decision.

I was later asked to join the meeting. The Commission's verdict was that, in the event of a protest, it would be upheld as the commissioners were not satisfied that the carburettors were in accordance with the regulations. In view of the fact that we had discussed matters in such a friendly and frank atmosphere, and bearing in mind the discrepancy of English and French texts, they then made the remarkable proposal that we should change the carburettors before the Monte-Vals-Monte leg. I said that this would be quite impossible because even if our crews could make up enough time to have the work done, we had not got any other carburettors with us. Furthermore, I said I thought that it would be a scandalous thing to do as it would be totally against the event regulations and would undoubtedly give rise to justified protests from other competitors. It was also putting the organisers into an even more embarrassing position as, having allowed us to start, the Commission now wanted us to 'secretly' change the specification of our engines.

The atmosphere was becoming somewhat strained. The Commission then offered us the opportunity of changing the carburettors in parc ferme overnight. This proposal was even more ridiculous than the first so I reminded the commissioners that the whole purpose of our discussion was to try and avoid a repetition of the 1966 drama and not to end up with an even bigger fiasco!

The tone of the meeting became evident when I was given what was clearly a bogus telephone message that Paddy Hopkirk was in the parc ferme at this very moment trying to change the carburettors on his car. What had I got to say about that? I looked across the table at the RAC Steward, our good friend Jack Kemsley, in sheer amazement and it was he who suggested that we all go down to the parc ferme right away to witness whether Paddy was as good a mechanic as he was a driver! The humour was not appreciated by the French but I think we won that round as that particular matter was quickly forgotten!

Continuing the argument, I was adamant that our cars complied with whatever translation of the regulations chosen. I again refused to change

1967 to 1970: THE END OF THE LINE by Peter Browning

the carburettors and, in a clearly hostile atmosphere, said that I must now consider withdrawing the team. Following discussions with the drivers, opinion was divided about whether they should stick their necks out on the Common Run and the Mountain Circuit only to face the chance of disqualification, or withdraw now and save the cars for another event. It was a difficult decision and it was by no means unanimous that, after yet another meeting with the Sporting Commission, we decided to press on. That final meeting had at least revealed that the Monte organisers would not raise any objections or disqualify us but would have to carefully consider the reasons presented by anyone who lodged an official protest. This, we thought, was fair enough and would be the end of the matter as it was clear that all of our rivals agreed with our interpretation of the regulations.

With the Rally over, the cars were taken to the usual scrutineering but our suspicions were aroused when instead of asking for just the class-winning car, the scrutineers demanded to see all three Minis. Heading the scrutineering team was the same gentleman who had been officiating in 1966, and clearly he was still very anti-Mini. He certainly did not agree with the Sporting Commission's decision that the carburettors complied with the regulations. The carburettors and the manifolds were torn apart to try and find some slight discrepancy with the regulations or the homologation sheet. This dogmatic but ultimately unsuccessful exercise took so long that, by the time the scrutineering session was over, there was insufficient time for even a cursory glance at the winning Porsche!

Happily none of the competitors protested so the results stood; the matter was finally resolved by sending formal applications to the FIA which ultimately agreed that our interpretation of the regulations was correct and that the carburettors were quite legal. It was a nightmare situation which I certainly did not need on top of trying to ensure that all other aspects of our team operation went according to plan.

Pushing our luck

I experienced many occasions where the special determination of crews and mechanics brought success, such as when Paddy Hopkirk took second place on the 1967 Rally of the Flowers in Italy after his Mini mysteriously managed to freewheel the final 20km of the rally with a broken transmission!

Paddy came off the end of the final stage of the rally up in the mountains behind San Remo with no drive, and no time to investigate or repair the problem. Doug Watts (Foreman) and I were servicing at the end of the stage in a Princess R 'barge' expecting only to have to do a quick 'wash and polish' before the final run down to the coast road and the finish. The ever-resourceful Doug immediately decided that Paddy should try and freewheel to the finish and we would push the car with the barge where necessary. We set off down a steep descent and did not have to give the Mini too many taps on the rear bumper. However, a passage control halfway down the section presented a problem because, clearly, we could not be seen to be giving assistance. Just before the control we gave Paddy a healthy push and he was able to coast into the control, blipping the engine to simulate a slipping clutch. We had to hold back while the marshals stamped the time card and then, fortunately, the marshals and some spectators gave the ailing Mini a helping hand down the road which was downhill again, thankfully.

As we got closer to the coast more and more photographers had gathered at this section to get pictures of the cars, so when they came in sight we had to back off while Paddy coasted by, blipping the throttle and giving them a smile and a wave as if he had slowed down to let them get a good shot!

When we reached the coast road it was dead flat with some 2km to go before the final control. We certainly got some very strange looks from drivers when the Mini shot past them seemingly towing this lumbering saloon! The final drama occurred as we approached the control which was located after a short tunnel at a T junction. Doug built up speed in the tunnel and ejected the Mini into the T junction where Paddy did a handbrake left turn into the control and we went right to hide! Paddy did a great job, having just enough momentum to reach the control and feigning clutch slip all the way to impress the waiting TV crews and press. Paddy's second place had been salvaged! The only one to question how the Mini had managed to go so far with no transmission was John Davenport, co-driver of the third placed Lancia driven by Ove Andersson!

SPECIAL TUNING

Establishment of the Special Tuning Department, which also came under the control of the Comps Manager, was a big step forward. Before Special Tuning private owners had to order parts through their local dealer, most of whom did not know anything about competitions and were not generally interested in small one-off orders. More importantly they were seldom able to cope with the inevitable panic call from the often stranded competitor. Those who knew the ropes used to call at Abingdon and see our ever-helpful storeman Neville Challis, who would take pity on them (often out of hours) and hand over the parts to save the day. And as there was not really a system set up for payment this was quite a financial drain on the budget.

Special Tuning changed all that and, under the direction of Basil Wales, we could not only ensure that an adequate supply of competition parts was available, but customers could come to Abingdon and get them over the counter in the usual way. The Department also extended the business with its own workshops and mechanics to prepare cars (mainly for overseas distributors), which left the Comps Shop free to concentrate on preparation of the works cars.

It was pertinent that when BL closed us down it made a positive move to keep the ST Department going, despite my assertion that without Comps winning and developing the parts ST was unlikely to last long – and I was right. The sad thing was that by the time BL closed us down the profit from ST (possibly around £250,000) was more or less covering our annual Comps budgets, so in essence Comps activity was not costing the company anything!

BONUS SCHEME

A Competitions Manager should always try and keep an eye open for up and coming driving talent, and I very soon discovered there was no shortage of young drivers who felt that they only needed one chance to get behind the wheel of a works car to prove their talent. The keener ones would turn up at the works, often unannounced, to take you out to lunch and persuade you to give them some support. One's worst fears were realised when they tried to prove their driving skills on the run through the country lanes to our favourite watering hole, The Dog House at Frilford Heath. Even worse was the drive home after a few beers; I always tried to arrange to be in the driving seat!

The introduction of the BMC Bonus Scheme – which paid out money to those who gained success (at home and overseas) in specified events – was the saviour to this situation. Thereafter many private owners were instructed to: "Go out and prove your potential in your own car and at your own level within the sport, and if you are successful you will be financially rewarded."

At the end of the season a review of what was paid out under the Bonus Scheme gave a very clear picture of promising up-and-coming hopefuls. And they did not have to buy me lunch!

LEYLAND RULE

The Minis running out of steam against the European opposition coincided with the change in management to BL, and could not have happened at a worse time. The BL people were generally not competition-minded and did not take kindly to our lack of success. Many of the top brass were ex-Triumph people who had memories of expensive and not-too-successful Triumph competitions activities in more recent times.

However, to be fair, I was allowed a roving commission to go and talk to management at the various divisions about competition potential and, as such, was perhaps in a unique position within this massive corporation. Looking back I probably was not the right man to be doing this because discussing technical matters was certainly not my scene.

The European opposition at the time was building-in homologation options at the design stage of the car, which resulted in highly competitive entries from Porsche, Ford, Renault-Alpine and Lancia. I could not get across to the people at BL that to compete we had to do the same and, most importantly, make a long-term commitment. But everyone was struggling to meet production deadlines to tight budgets and, to be fair, they probably did not need the distraction of considering competition

1967 to 1970: THE END OF THE LINE by Peter Browning

options – and they certainly did not welcome this young upstart from Abingdon pushing them for action! Mind you, when you start with a car like the Allegro and Marina there's not much hope!

And when we did compete with 'their' cars BL was insistent that its engineering people were totally involved in what went on. An example was preparation of the Triumph 2.5PI cars for the London to Mexico Marathon in 1970 when we began with an extensive testing programme at the Bagshot Military Testing Ground, and gradually honed the car into reliable shape. But every modification we made (and there were a great many) was meant to have engineering approval from Coventry. This, of course, couldn't happen when we realised that we would never get the job done. You break the suspension on Monday, come up with a solution on Tuesday, fix it on Wednesday and go testing on Thursday; there simply is not time to consult the designers, get budget approval for the mod, wait for a drawing and a part number, and then hang about waiting for someone to provide the new part.

One of the joys of working within the Abingdon factory was the total support from top management and the head of every department – and if you wanted expert design advice there were people like Syd Enever, Terry Mitchell and Don Hayter always available from the MG Development Department next door. And these were people who knew about competitions and could come up with the right answers – and quickly!

Working with BL

The concept of BL was to bring together the various manufacturing groups and to rationalise model production and other aspects of marketing. As an example, someone from MG Development told me that typical of the plans was that every BL car should have exactly the same door locks so that the price could be slashed to the minimum. Unfortunately this was the era of militant strike action within the industry and things like this played right into the hands of the strike force; one lorry driver from Willmot Breeden who went on strike for a longer lunch break could have brought BL car production to a standstill if there were no door locks.

In my travels around the various companies, when I was given a free hand to try and evaluate the current and future model range for competitions, I found actually very little evidence of everyone working toward the corporate objective. There was still strong marque allegiance between Rover, Triumph, MG and Austin/Morris which I visited; I was told, incidentally, not to go to Jaguar ...

I understood that all of the Chief Engineers and their henchman sat on a central BL Design Committee, presumably so that the corporate new model policy could be discussed. But on my travels it was clear to me that all sorts of behind-closed-doors projects were still going on which certain parties did not want anyone to know about. In hindsight this was probably one of the reasons why my inquisitive enquiries were not sympathetically received ...

The Marathons

It was on reflection – and perhaps not a bad thing – that the BL formation coincided with the era of the Marathons: London to Sydney in 1968 and London to Mexico in 1970. At a time when we were certainly struggling with the Minis on World Championship rallies, the Marathons – unique events demanding different aspects of car preparation, driving challenge and back-up service and support – did give us a chance to look at using other models within the BL range.

The other advantage was that Marathon budgets were set aside from the annual Competitions budget, and although pretty hefty (probably around £100,000 an event), a fair chunk of the charges was shared by BL divisions overseas. This was certainly the case on the London to Sydney where BMC Australia provided and paid for the very extensive service and back-up in Australia. Also it was clear that BL management could more closely relate to the worldwide promotional value of the Marathons rather than the more restricted benefits of World Championship rallying.

For London to Sydney our directive from the PR people was to use the 1800 which, at first, did not seem a very exciting prospect. However, we did not really have any option and had done quite a bit of work with the 1800 on previous events. Most significant was the fact that BMC Australia was aggressively marketing the 1800 at the time.

The big decision on the Marathons was whether to go two- or three-up;

the benefit of it being more relaxing for the crew to go three-up (with the third man also usually acting as riding mechanic) had to be balanced against the disadvantage of the extra weight. For London to Sydney the 1800 certainly had room for three, and we finally proved that the suspension could handle the extra load (with some late engineering help from BMC in Australia). We did not think the results would be decided on close stage times (and this proved to be the case) – long distance reliability seemed vital. The crews made the decision to go three-up.

Paddy Hopkirk finishing runner-up to Marcus' Hunter driven by Andrew Cowan on London to Sydney was a disappointing result after all the effort, but at least all five works 1800s finished. However, Lord Stokes was desperately disappointed that we did not win.

When London to Mexico came around two years later I obviously pitched to make an entry on the basis that we were still not making any headway with rally Mini development. This time there was a little more enthusiasm from the strong Triumph fraternity within BL when we suggested using the Triumph 2.5PI. We had already had some promising experience of the car on rough events like the Scottish and the RAC Rallies.

Our budget was barely adequate and, with very little back-up support promised in South America, we had to plan to fend for ourselves in most regions. My old mate Brian Culcheth offered to do the complete South American recce (with Johnstone Syer) and they did a great job analysing the competitive 'primes', locating service points and booking hotels, etc. Interestingly, Brian came home with the firm decision that after London to Sydney he would go two-up whilst all the others in the team opted for three-up again.

After a great deal of discussion we came to the conclusion that the only logistical and financially viable way to move mechanics and spares around South America would be by air, so we needed a big plane. I got on the phone to various airlines and finally did a deal with British Caledonian for the use of a Britannia to cover the whole event. I don't think any rally team had ever set off with such an impressive service plan!

Brian's recce experience, and the fact that he made the right decision to go two-up, paid off and he did well to finish runner-up to the very much faster and lighter Escort of Hannu Mikkola. However, it was still another 'second best' performance that I had to try and explain to a now even more frustrated Lord Stokes.

Range Rover for the Marathon

In preparation for the London to Mexico Marathon we heard about the then-to-be-announced Range Rover which, on paper, sounded like an eminently suitable car for this event. I called Ralph Nash at Rover who, though ever-cautious, at least invited me up to the works to discuss the idea. I took Doug Watts and Geoff Mabbs with me in the hope that we might be able to have a test run in the car.

Obviously when we saw one of the pre-production prototypes we thought that it would be very competitive; probably not as quick as some of the opposition but hopefully a reliable and tough finisher. I tried to persuade the Rover men that it would be a super promotion for the new model but I don't really think they were too keen on Abingdon playing with their new toy. After some persuasion Ralph at least said that we could borrow the car for a quick test run on the strict proviso that we did not expose it too openly to the public and, of course, that we did not damage it!

Our first mistake was to stop for a bite of lunch at a pub on the way to the local Girling test track. We left the car in the pub car park but, unfortunately, had chosen the pub where the Rover directors had their lunch. They had a fit when they looked out of the window and saw the car surrounded by interested onlookers!

Finding out who had borrowed the car and what we were planning they decided to join us at the airfield after lunch. Somewhat embarrassed we all stood on the inside of one of the corners while Geoff set off for a few laps of the airfield perimeter. Everything went okay until Geoff approached the bend where we were all standing which, unbeknown to him, tightened deceptively and had a nasty ditch on the outside. As the lumbering Range Rover approached at unabated speed I feared the worst. At the last moment Geoff realised the danger, the big car went into a monumental slide and, with brakes locked and smoking tyres,

1967 to 1970: THE END OF THE LINE by Peter Browning

left the tarmac, cleared the ditch and landed – thankfully the right way up – in the middle of the field. I can see the car now – one headlight unit hanging out by the wire, a whiff of steam escaping from under the bonnet, and Geoff struggling to get out with the collapsed headlining wrapped around his head.

Geoff nonchalantly alighted, surveyed the damage and walked across to the assembled shocked party muttering: "Not bad, but you've got to cure that bump steer!" Needless to say we did not take the Range Rover on the Marathon!

Racing Coopers

One of the first budget cuts to come under BL was the instruction for me to terminate the long-term agreements with the Cooper Car Company racing Minis in the British Saloon Car Championship, and the Donald Healey Motor Company racing Austin-Healeys in World Championship sports car races.

As far as Healey was concerned this virtually put out of business its racing shop at Warwick under Geoff Healey, as its funding had come from our Competitions budget. I had to make the announcement at the celebration dinner after Le Mans in 1968 which did not exactly go down too well. Withdrawal of further support for Coopers was coupled with the proposal that Abingdon would now take over the Mini racing programme. Whilst I knew that this was going to be a tough assignment for the team, and probably not too popular amongst the basically rallying fraternity, it did at least give us an ongoing programme with a budget for another season at a time when there was very little else in the pipeline.

I had in fact suggested to BL that if we contested the 1300cc class I could possibly get Coopers to go for the 1000cc class, so that we would stage a two-pronged attack on the British Championship. Predictably, when I discussed this with John Cooper he, always the gentleman, politely said that he was not too keen and would like to continue with a newly sponsored 1300 team. I know that he was very upset at losing the long-term agreement through Abingdon, and feared it would not be long before he lost his royalties on Mini-Cooper production. I think he relished the chance of continuing to fly the flag for the Cooper Car Company.

The result therefore was that we had the two Mini teams in the 1300 class (John Rhodes/John Handley for Abingdon and Gordon Spice/Steve Neal for Cooper) who spent the whole of the season racing against each other after losing sight of the objective which was to beat the Escorts! To be honest we could never have beaten the Escorts anyway, and it ended up with Abingdon trying to prove it could build a race Mini as good as the Coopers while the Coopers had to try and thrash the 'works' cars! The only saving grace was that the racing budget was a mere fraction of what we had been spending on rallying, and it kept us in business for another season.

Rallycross

When TV started to screen rallycross on Saturday afternoons I saw this as a possibly not-too-difficult or extravagant publicity opportunity which would, perhaps, impress BL. It was also a convenient way to use the old rally Minis. What we did not account for was the strength of the opposition in the form of club Mini drivers who had been at it for a long time, and had developed cars to a competitive specification that was way beyond the rather conservative Abingdon approach.

Still, we did have some success when we drafted in the talents of John Rhodes, John Handley and Brian Culcheth, which at least gave the BL directors something to talk about in the boardroom lunch on Monday.

Ironically, one of the few times that anyone from Longbridge ever called us to say 'well done' was when we entered Geoff Mabbs in a totally standard-looking Rover. Geoff wore a pinstripe suit and Murray Walker even commented on the copy of the *Financial Times* rolled up on the rear parcel shelf!

Support at the Top

I know that Marcus and Stuart would agree when I say that it is absolutely essential for the Competitions Manager to have the support of senior management to fight your corner when things don't go according to plan. John Thornley, as MG's General Manager, was instrumental in setting up the Competitions Department in the first place in 1955 under Marcus, and remained to support both Stuart and myself. John knew all about racing and rallying and, as far as I was concerned, always ensured that the right people were aware of our successes. Equally importantly he was able to explain our failures to those who may not have appreciated the things that can rob you of success. I was very sad to hear of his early retirement from Abingdon through ill health and in particular when we needed support to fight our cause against BL – not only in respect of Competitions but, more seriously, the ultimate closure of MG.

Explaining our failures to BL was a painful experience which I certainly did not enjoy, principally because I found myself talking to people who probably did not believe in what we were trying to achieve in the first place, and certainly did not understand that money alone does not buy success.

My worst experience of this was the case of the Corsican fan belts in 1967. BMC in France was keen for us to try and win the Tour de Corse which, at the time, was a significant event for the company to promote. We had a big budget, built two very quick Minis, and the crews spent a lot of expensive time doing a thorough recce, virtually making pace notes for the entire route.

A few kilometres into the first stage both cars suffered from slipping fan belts and terminal overheating problems as a result. Obviously there was a serious inquest into why this happened; the belts were, of course, routinely checked and tightened before the start. It was of little consolation when we got home to find that the manufacturer had supplied us with a batch of duff belts. Explaining that to the top brass on Monday morning was not easy!

Racing Rover

As a bit of a last ditch attempt to try and impress BL with a result, and in the knowledge that we were clutching at straws now, the idea of the racing Rover was born – on the basis that there is usually no substitute for sheer power!

I met up with Bill Shaw in 1970 and he agreed to build an out-and-out lightweight Rover racer fitted with a fully modified 4.3 litre Traco V8 power unit. Bill did a fantastic job in a very short space of time, Roy Pierpoint was the chosen driver and, after some brief tests at Castle Combe, performance was certainly impressive if reliability unknown.

It was decided to put in a late entry for the 86 Hour Marathon at the Nürburgring where a works Mini had also been entered. The event was run on the full circuit and on the opening lap the Rover had such an enormous lead over all the works Porsches and the other serious opposition that everyone thought that an accident must be delaying all the other cars. For the first hour the Rover continued to pull out an amazing lead over the opposition, then we calmed the pace a bit and the drivers were able to relax making only one gear change per lap!

The Rover was the sensation of the event when, unfortunately, at 15 hours a serious prop shaft vibration began and for safety reasons it was decided to withdraw the car rather than risk an accident. At the time the Rover was three laps in the lead which, around the 'Ring, was impressive! However, there was little point in getting too excited as while the Rover was making headlines, BL had already announced the closure of the Competitions Department back home.

Finale

The final BL management decision to close the Department was really drawn out over a period of months. At a series of meetings, mainly with George Turnbull, who I found to be an extremely pleasant and sympathetic chap, the inevitable decision was made on the basis that, given the current range of BL models, we really could not hope to continue to be competitive with the opposition of the day.

More significantly, despite all of the discussions with the various divisions, there was clearly no way the cash strapped companies desperately concentrating on maintaining production and dwindling sales could be persuaded into considering our need for the homologation of serious competition options on existing or, more practically, new models.

By this time we had reached the stage of there being no annual competitions budget; budget approval was given for specific individual projects and each event had to be justified. Unless we were in with a chance of success, or on the rare occasion that the local dealer was prepared to foot all or part of the bill, the budget was not approved.

The final policy instruction regarding the closure of Comps, which was issued to the then MG

1967 to 1970: THE END OF THE LINE by Peter Browning

management, meant the earliest release of drivers and co-drivers from their contracts, and disposal of the existing fleet of competition cars. The staff and the mechanics were offered production jobs within the MG factory – some took up the offer; others left Abingdon to look for new opportunities within the motor trade. Experiencing feelings of guilt in letting the team down and failing to save the day, I was forced to resign when it was made clear to me that BL did not want me around to make uncomplimentary comments to the press. I remember being incensed that no-one from BL came to Abingdon to personally make the announcement to the team (or the MG management at the time). I felt this was unforgivable bearing the mind the team's heritage of past achievements.

THE SPIRIT LIVES ON

Throughout the years of BMC Competitions the main outstanding team quality was the genuine loyalty and friendship of those involved. Most of the mechanics were local people born and bred, and they and their families formed a close-knit community, irrespective of their position within the Department. The drivers and co-drivers were welcomed into that community when they worked together and got to know each other on events. This unique team spirit was demonstrated on so many occasions.

The strength of that spirit lives on today and since the closure of Comps we have organised a regular BMC Competitions Reunion Dinner which is attended by former drivers, co-drivers, mechanics, management and staff involved, plus supporting trade personnel. They still come from the far corners of the world to meet up with old friends.

The interest in the achievements of the team is reflected in the fact that, in the 50 years since Comps was started in 1955, probably more has been written about the BMC works cars, the mechanics and the drivers than any other team. We hope that this book will have filled in one or two gaps in the story of what was unquestionably one of the most successful teams of all time during a period generally recognised as the golden era of rallying.

Visit Veloce on the web – www.veloce.co.uk
Details of all our books • Newsletter • New book news • Special offers

THE BRITISH MOTOR CORPORATION

Competitions Department

ABINGDON-ON-THAMES, BERKSHIRE

TELEPHONE: ABINGDON 251   TELEGRAMS: EMGEE, ABINGDON   TELEX: 83128

TO: ALL MEMBERS OF THE BMC TEAM

While we are all aware of the likely outcome of the current meetings with British Leyland concerning the future of the Competitions Department, I feel that we must all be very careful what we say to the press and to other influencial people at the present time.

Already there have been some untimely and ill-informed comments in the technical press which could well jeopardize the chances of a favourable outcome to our meetings at Longbridge.

The present situation is as follows and you are free to pass this information on to anyone interested.

It is established that the Competitions Department will continue in its present form at Abingdon although our future activities are likely to be restricted to those events in which we stand a very good chance of winning outright, or those events which bring exceptional publicity benefits at home or overseas.

Our future programme is to be agreed at a meeting at Longbridge on the 5th August. This meeting will agree the programme for the next financial year commencing 1st August, 1968 (although it seems certain that our entries in the 1000 Lakes Rally and the Nurburgring Marathon will not be affected). However, our participation in the RAC Rally, the London - Sydney Marathon and the Monte Carlo Rally is by no means definite.

The situation is further aggravated with the production problems at Abingdon and at the moment I have no indication of when this will be resolved and when our shop can return to full-time competitions work.

Until such time as Longbridge decides our future programme and Abingdon resolves its production difficulties, you will appreciate that I am in no position to make any decision about our competition activities after the 1000 Lakes Rally and the Nurburgring Marathon.

I am sure that you will agree that at a time when our future depends on 'winning' it would be wrong for us to enter any event unless we are confident that we have the time to do so fully prepared in every aspect to our very highest standards.

Peter Browning,
Competitions Manager

As early as spring 1968 when this was written and I had been in the hot seat for only a few months, there was clearly already concern about the future of the Competitions Department under the impending BL management. The reference to the production problems at the factory alluded to the occasional request (when we were not too busy) for the mechanics to help out with rectification problems. For example, when a large batch of cars came off the production line and were found to have faulty water pumps, they had all to be changed before dispatch, and a rally mechanic could do the job in quarter of the time taken by a line worker! Helping in this way was a good bit of PR for the Department within the factory.

1967 to 1970: THE END OF THE LINE by Peter Browning

THE BRITISH MOTOR CORPORATION
Competitions Department
ABINGDON-ON-THAMES, BERKSHIRE

TELEPHONE: ABINGDON 251   TELEGRAMS: EMGEE, ABINGDON   TELEX: 83128

From:
Mr. P. W. Browning

To:
H. Liddon   R. Aaltonen
J. M. Wood   T. Makinen
P. Easter   P. Hopkirk
E. Green   R. A. Fall

This is to bring you up-to-date with the latest plans. I have entered five 1800s and nominated the following crews: Makinen/Easter, Aaltonen/Liddon, Fall/Wood, Hopkirk/A.N. Other, Evan Green/Jack Murray (BMC Australia entry).

It was my original plan to send Liddon off on recce around 23 June and for Wood and Easter to catch up with him in Belgrade. For the following reasons the recce car will not be ready to leave until the middle of July:-

a) We only received our first Mark II 1800 this week and I think it essential that we use a Mark II on the recce because there are many detailed improvements.

b) I want the recce car to be prepared mechanically exactly as the rally cars will be, this means a complete strip down to the bare metal to strengthen the body and lighten as appropriate. This will take time but I feel there is no point in setting out on the recce with a car which is not armour plated as we intend to use it on the event.

c) From Australia we are getting details of the larger rear hydrolastic units which they use on the 1800 Pick-up. This means a major re-build on the back end which again will take us some time, but I feel that the recce car must have this modification.

d) We also want to fit the steel couplings used on the Wolseley automatic and this may mean special drive shafts which could delay things, but again I feel these items must be tested on the recce car.

Even working flat out the car cannot be ready until mid-July, so I now suggest the following recce plans:-

As soon as possible after the Acropolis Liddon, Easter and Aaltonen will return to Abingdon for a post mortem on Acropolis 1800 problems (Aaltonen is

---

General planning notes to the team regarding the 1800 entries for the London to Sydney Marathon. Interesting that my view at this time was to go two-up when, in the end, everyone decided to go three-up!

2.

asked to come with me to Dunlops on 6 June to talk about wider section tyres for rally use). Fall will be able to report on his 1800 experiences on the Shell 4000 by the second week in June.

I therefore suggest that Liddon and Wood leave with the recce 1800 on 15 July arriving Bombay around 29 July. Liddon then flies to Freemantle and meets Green with an Australian prepared recce 1800 and completes the Australian leg arriving Sydney around 7 August and flies home around 9 August. Wood flies from Bombay around 31 July having left the 1800 with BMC dealer.

Easter and whoever goes with Hopkirk then fly out to Bombay around 1 August with the necessary spares to re-build the 1800 in conjunction with local BMC dealer. They then drive over the route in the reverse direction, arriving home around 15 August.

This will leave Wood available to do the Alpine route notes during early August. The delayed start to the recce will also give everyone more time to get their visas sorted out and for the necessary injections.

The above arrangements insure that one representative from our team with the exception of Evan Green has covered the London - Bombay leg while Liddon will have done the complete run and will be able to insure a consistency of route note making for the entire trip.

Summary of the time abroad therefore looks as follows:

<u>Liddon</u>: 15 July - 9 August. Drive London - Bombay, fly Bombay - Freemantle, drive Freemantle - Sydney, fly Sydney - London.

<u>Wood</u>: 15 July - 29 July. Drive London - Bombay, fly Bombay - London.
5 - 15 August. Alpine route note recce.

<u>Easter & Hopkirk's co-driver</u>: 1 - 15 August. Fly London - Bombay, drive Bombay - London.

As soon as possible I would welcome your comments as to whether you feel you want a two or three man crew, my view is that all of you are now fully trained in re-building 1800s in the field and well qualified to cope with most problems. I feel that the weight of the extra person is a considerable disadvantage, particularly with the 1800 suspension problems. The cost of providing riding mechanics is considerable and I feel that the money could be better spent in having Abingdon mechanics servicing en route.

Liddon has already submitted a useful list of suggestions, all of which will be incorporated in the recce car. If anyone else has any suggestions for modifications or special equipment please pass them on to me or Douggie Watts.

PWB/MS
23.5.68

BMC Competitions Department Secrets ...

THE BRITISH MOTOR CORPORATION

Competitions Department

ABINGDON-ON-THAMES, BERKSHIRE

TELEPHONE: ABINGDON 251 TELEGRAMS: EMGEE, ABINGDON TELEX: 83128

PWB/SL

Memo to: T. Makinen/P. Easter
          R. Aaltonen/H. Liddon
          P. Hopkirk/T. Nash
          T. Fall/M. Wood
          E. Green/J. Murray/G. Shephert

5th September, 1968

LONDON-SYDNEY MARATHON

Following a meeting with Sir Donald Stokes last week I have at last received his agreement to go ahead with five works entries in the Marathon.

Entries have been made for the crews named above and, while we still have time to nominate the third crew members, would you please liason with your co-driver and decide as soon as possible upon your third man if you wish to go three up.

Reservations have been made for all crews to fly Sydney to London on the organisers special charter flight on Sunday, 22nd December. This saves us about £700 over the regular flights. If you do not wish to return home on this flight will you please let me know by the 13th September at the very latest otherwise you will be charged with the cancellation fee of £25. If you decide not to return home on the charter flight you will have to make your own travel arrangements direct with Stan Sibthorpe of MAT. You will be charged with any expenditure above the charter flight fare of £190.

As I have had to submit the lowest possible budget to Sir Donald to receive approval to enter this event, in view of the very large prize fund the usual arrangements for prize money and bonus will be changed for this event. We will take 50% of the money as a contribution towards the organising costs, the remaining 50% will be divided 10% to the mechanics fund and the rest split between the crew.

Adjustments will also be made to the regular day money payments for the duration of the event when it will obviously be impossible to spend the usual £12 per day allowance on the road and the boat reservations paid by us include full board. Each crew member will therefore receive only £5 per day. Each car will, of course, have an adequate emergency float and petrol money. This will save well over £2000 which will be set aside to cover improved service facilities.

I am sorry if these measures seem a little hard but I can assure you that Sir Donald was not at all enthusiastic about our participation in the Marathon and had we not already been committed to considerable expense on the recce and produced a very tight budget, I have no doubt that he would have withdrawn the whole team.

Peter Browning.

Confirmation of the agreed London to Sydney Marathon entries and a very clear indication that the bean counters at Longbridge would be keeping a close watch on the budget! The reduction in the usually generous subsistence allowance was not well received! The final paragraph confirms that I got a severe ticking-off for having already (deliberately!) authorized the recces and preparation of the cars to go ahead before the final budget was approved in the belief that BL was unlikely to withdraw the entries at that late stage!

1967 to 1970: THE END OF THE LINE by Peter Browning

THE BRITISH MOTOR CORPORATION
Competitions Department
ABINGDON-ON-THAMES, BERKSHIRE

TELEPHONE: ABINGDON 251   TELEGRAMS: EMGEE, ABINGDON   TELEX: 83128

LONDON - SYDNEY MARATHON, 1968

The following works entries have been accepted - all in Mark II 1800s:-

    Makinen/Easter
    Aaltonen/Liddon
    Hopkirk/Nash
    Fall/Wood
    Green/Murray

We have the option to nominate additional crew members later.

The following was agreed with Liddon, Easter, Nash and Fall at Abingdon on 12 June:

Recce

The leaving date for the recce was brought forward to Wednesday 10 July. Liddon, Easter and Nash will cover the London - Bombay leg, departing Dover on 10 July at 11.30, arriving Boulogne 13.00, drive to Bombay, arriving by 31 July.

They will be met by one Abingdon mechanic and Wood who fly London - Bombay on 30 July (flight BA.778) departing 12.15, arriving Bombay 04.30 (31st), to complete a full technical report on the car and, with the assistance of the local dealer, prepare the car for the return journey.

Liddon flies Bombay - Perth, Easter and Nash fly Bombay - London (all open-dated tickets) around 1 August.

Wood and mechanic drive Bombay - London, probably leaving around 4 August and arriving home around 24 August.

Green to meet Liddon in Perth on 1 August with Australian-prepared recce 1800 and after attending local Championship rally on 3/4 August leave for recce of Perth - Sydney leg arriving Sydney around 10 August. Liddon flies Sydney - London around 12 August (open-dated ticket).

Notes on Recce

Liddon to work out detailed recce schedule and advise Browning as soon as possible so that visas and road permits can be obtained.

Everyone to be responsible for getting their vaccinations done in time, you require the following: smallpox, yellow fever, cholera, plague and typhus.

Recce Car Preparation (in addition to build sheet notes already agreed with Watts).

Three spot lamps on front, one mounted high up in centre. One wing mounted spot light (Safari type) mounted on co-driver's wing - as near the windscreen as possible.

This bulletin shows the entry details accepted by the organisers, although crew nominations changed continuously mainly as decided by the co-drivers' 'mafia'. I purposely did not have much input in this decision on the basis that the co-drivers (and particularly those who had done the recces) had the best picture of what was going to be involved, they all worked as a team and the objective was to have crews that got on well together. My only comment was that at least one member of the crew ought to be able act as 'mechanic' in the event of problems.

2.

Driver's seat as used on Acropolis recce car.
Co-driver's seat long back Mini recliner.
Centre rear seat with foot rest between front seats.

Centre mounted grab handles beneath rear screen instead of the pair on wings as on Safari.

Supply pair of chains as tried by Makinen on Safari for preventing rear wheel mud clogging.

Twin spare wheels mounted on roof at front in lockable box. Spares inside rather than on the roof if possible.

Fit rubber bladed cooling fan on dashboard.

Carry two spare tyres and four spare tubes.

Safari type winch with one lightweight dural stake. Same cable length as on Safari.
Two nylon tow ropes.

No under-bonnet or boot lights but good lead lamp.

Lap and diagonal seat belts for all three crew members.

Provide ice box to carry drink and food.

BMC Competitions Department Secrets ...

THE BRITISH MOTOR CORPORATION

Competitions Department

ABINGDON-ON-THAMES, BERKSHIRE

TELEPHONE: ABINGDON 251   TELEGRAMS: EMGEE, ABINGDON   TELEX: 83138

PWB/SL   4th October, 1968

Memo to: R. Aaltonen/H. Liddon/C. Baker
           T. Fall/M. Wood/B. Culcheth
           P. Hopkirk/T. Nash
           E. Green/J. Murray/G. Shepheard
           Kingsley/Bell/Evans

LONDON TO SYDNEY MARATHON

Injections

It is your own responsibility to ensure that you have the necessary injections and medical certificates. The minimum requirement is to have innoculations against Cholera, Smallpox and TAB and we also suggest in addition you are covered against Polio, Yellow Fever, Plague and TAB 'T'.

Visas

If you haven't already done so, would you please let us have your passport so that we can obtain the necessary visas. Those who have already been on the London to Bombay run must check that their old visas are still valid.

Fire Arms

Suggest that it would be a wise precaution for each car to carry a small fire arm for some personal protection in the event of a breakdown or accident in remote parts. As most members of the team have already demonstrated their prowess at this art in the past, I am leaving each crew to make their own arrangements for the supply of suitable armoury! We will not provide gun slings on the roof I hasten to add. A small pistol which can be conveniently located under cover in the car is what we have in mind.

Return Flight

As the organisers of the charter flight are demanding full payment now and they have indicated that we are going to have to forfeit the full cost of the tickets if we make a cancellation, I have reserved only six places on the special charter flight home from Sydney to London on the 22nd December, these we will fill with those who wish to come home immediately. The rest will have open dated return tickets and will have to pay any excess if they wish to return home by a longer route or break their journey.

Chusan accommodation

I have booked twin berth port hole cabins with private showers on the Chusan as follows:
          P. Hopkirk/T. Nash
          R. Aaltonen/H. Liddon
          T. Fall/M. Wood
          B. Culcheth/C. Baker
          E. Green/J. Murray
          T. Kingsley/D. Bell
          P. Evans/G. Shepheard

Some final instructions for London to Sydney. I am not sure who instigated the bit about carrying firearms but am sure that nobody did so in the end! Interesting that even at this late stage the crews have changed again. Timo Makinen dropped out of the line-up with the comment that he could think of a lot better things to do for a month than drive an 1800 to Australia!

London-Sydney Marathon continued.   2

Hotel reservations on the event will be arranged as above pairings.

Baggage

The organisers are arranging for baggage to be put aboard the Chusan before she leaves Southampton. This will be in early November. I suggest that each crew takes one suit case containing clothing required on the boat and for the Australian leg. I will let you know details of the date of sailing as soon as I have them.

We are planning to give the crews at least two changes of clothing on the London-Bombay leg, probably at Belgrade and Kabul. This will necessitate the delivery of two sets of underwear, trousers, shirt, socks and handkerchieves a few days before the start.

Helmets

If you don't wish to use crash helmets at all on the event we will have intercoms fitted to a light-weight head set. We cannot consider using head sets for the London to Bombay leg for example and helmets in Australia because this will entail using two sets of intercom equipment so you either use helmets all the way or not at all. Would you please decide with you fellow crew members whether you wish to use helmets or not as soon as possible.

Blood Groups

The organisers have advised all competitors to carry a metal disc or bracelet on which their blood group is clearly engraved.

Peter Browning

1967 to 1970: THE END OF THE LINE by Peter Browning

SPECIAL TUNING PARTS
for the
848 c.c. & 998 c.c. MINI—997 c.c. & 998 c.c. MINI-COOPER

The following special items are available for the Mini and Mini Cooper.

They should be ordered through your nearest BMC Distributor, quoting the full Part Number and Prefix. See the appropriate Special Tuning Data Sheets or Booklet for any further details.

Description	Part No.	Qty./Car	Price each (£ s. d.)
BODYWORK			
Bonnet securing strap set	C-AJJ 3381	1	15 0
Wing extension kit, for 4½" wheels	C-AJJ 3316 A	1	4 17 6
Pivoting single lamp bracket	C-AJJ 3318	2	1 10 0
Competition 4-lamp mounting bar	C-AJJ 3329	1	5 5 0
Dash panels (R.H.D. Mk. I only)	C-AJJ 3330	1	3 0 0
Dash panels, pair (Mk. II only)	C-AJJ 3373	1	4 0 0
Perspex window set	C-AJJ 3363	1	15 0 0
Scottish Rally sump guard kit	C-AJJ 3320	1	30 0 0
BRAKES			
VG95 lined brake-shoes	C-8G 8997	4	1 9 2
VG95 linings and rivets	C-8G 8998	2	2 3 4
CRANKSHAFT, CLUTCH, AND FLYWHEEL			
Competition Tuftrided 848-c.c. crankshaft	C-AEG 515	1	15 0 0
Clutch driven plate	C-22G 247	1	3 2 6
Lightened steel flywheel	C-AEG 421	1	24 10 0
COOLER			
Competition type complete kit	C-AJJ 3309	1	10 5 0
DYNAMO PULLEY AND FAN			
Pulley for reduced speed	C-AEA 535	1	14 0
Fan belt to suit pulley C-AEA 535	C-AEA 756	1	8 0
Fan belt—short (use less dynamo)	C-AEA 539	1	10 0
Alternator mounting bracket	C-AHT 32	1	1 10 0
2-bladed fan	C-2A 997	2	3 3
EXHAUST			
Competition manifold	C-AEG 432	1	15 0 0
Competition exhaust system	C-ARA 334	1	15 0 0
FINAL DRIVE (See Sheet A-3 for other ratios)			
3·938 : 1 ratio—wheel	C-22G 340	1	4 0 0
pinion	C-22G 69	1	1 5 0
4·267 : 1 ratio—wheel (use with 22G 99)	C-22G 370	1	4 0 0
4·35 : 1 ratio—wheel (use with 22G 99)	C-22G 443	1	4 0 0
Primary gear kit (steel-backed brg.)	C-AJJ 3370	1	8 5 0
Crankshaft pulley locking plate	C-AHT 146	1	1 6
STAGE I TUNING KITS			
850-c.c. Manual gearbox only	C-AJJ 3343	1	44 0 0
848-c.c. Automatic gearbox only	C-AJJ 3345	1	46 0 0
998-c.c. Manual gearbox only	C-AJJ 3346	1	46 0 0
850-c.c. Automatic gearbox only	C-AJJ 3347	1	44 0 0
GEARBOX			
Cooper 'S' Std. ratio (straight cut):			
1st motion shaft	C-22G 427	1	3 15 0
3rd speed gear	C-22G 429	1	3 0 0
2nd speed gear	C-22G 428	1	3 10 0
Laygear	C-22G 335	1	5 10 0

This page from a Special Tuning leaflet illustrates the extensive range of parts available. This is an early leaflet as it says that parts had to be ordered through the local dealer; later, customers could come to Abingdon and buy direct.

BRITISH LEYLAND MOTOR CORPORATION

Competitions Department

ABINGDON-ON-THAMES, BERKSHIRE

TELEPHONE: ABINGDON 251   TELEGRAMS: EMGEE, ABINGDON   TELEX: 83128

TRIUMPH 2.5 P.I. RALLY CAR
RAC Rally - Group 2 Specification

Power Unit

6 cylinder 2498 cc OHV engine fitted with gas flowed cylinder head compression ratio 10.4:1, standard camshaft. Lucas petrol injection. Competition diaphragm spring clutch, 4 speed all synchromesh gearbox fitted with Laycock overdrive, Lucas alternator, oil cooler, special exhaust system terminating in front of o/s rear wheel.

Power output approx. 140 BHP.

Suspension/Brakes/Transmission

Normal suspension arrangements incorporating heavy duty Koni shock absorbers front and rear, uprated front and rear coil springs, 4.55:1 final drive ratio incorporating limited slip differential. Tandem master cylinder with Girling vacuum servo unit.
Anti fade brake material, Ferodo DS11 pads, VG95 rear shoes.
Road wheels - Magnesium alloy 13" x 7" fitted with Dunlop 195-70 x 13 SP44 Weathermaster tyres.

Body

Interior roll-over bar, special reclining co-drivers seat, fibreglass bucket drivers seat. 1 kg. dry powder fire extinguisher. Special jacking brackets fitted to body (2 each side) below door sills for hydraulic pillar jack. Twin quick release bonnet fasteners, Matt black bonnet, Special dished leather covered steering wheel. Full undershield protecting engine and gearbox. Auxiliary dash panels incorporating additional instruments, Halda Twin-Master and Heuer rally clocks.

Electrical

Quartz iodine twin headlamps, twin QI foglamps, battery condition gauge, auxiliary panel on gearbox tunnel incorporating all lamp switches and flexible map reading lamp. Electronic tachometer mounted on dash panel. Special Tudor heavy duty screenwasher. Overdrive switch incorporated in gear lever knob.

October, 1969.

This is the specification for the Triumph 2.5PI as entered for the Group 2 rallies (Scottish and RAC Rallies). The cars for London to Mexico were, of course, extensively modified, particularly in respect of suspension and body strengthening.

21.12.69.   Handling Tests on 2.5 MKII Triumph

Vehicle WJB189H   Circuit – Girling Test Ground Honiley

Drivers   Paddy Hopkirk   Brian Culcheth

Specification Test 'A'

    Front Springs   Prototype Stag with ½" packing
    Rear Springs   Innsbruk Estate with 1½" Packing
    Front Struts   Uprated Koni inserts – with Aeon Bump Rubbers
    Rear Dampers   Uprated Koni Type 82
    Castor Angle   RH 3°P   LH 3°P
    K.P.I.   "   14°   "   12°
    Camber Angle (Front) " 1½°N   " 1½°N
    Camber Angle (Rear)   " 0°   " ½°P
    Track   1/16" Toe-in Front and rear
    Weight (Total 3689 lb.) Front 1757 lb. Rear 1904 lb.

Driver's Comments:-

    Excessive initial understeer
    Transferring to wild oversteer on exit of corner
    Excessive body roll
    Wheels and tyres 5½" x 15" Minilite – 185 x 15 SP44
    Tyre pressures 35 PSI front and rear

Test 'B' – As Test 'A' Except

    Adjusted front camber to   RH 3°N   LH 1½°N

Driver's Comments:-

    Understeer reduced but still high
    Steering Heavy
    Body roll and oversteer as Test 'A'

Test 'C'

    As Test 'B' except
    Adjusted rear camber by Machining Spring Packing to 9/16"

    RH 1½°N   LH 1½°N

    Drivers Comments:-

    Oversteer more controllable – otherwise as Test 'B'

Test 'D'

    As Test 'C' Except

    LH Front Aeon Bump Rubber removed

Driver's Comments:-

    Car felt unbalanced

Test 'E' – As Test 'C' except:-

    Reduced castor angle to   RH 1½°   LH 2°
    Re-checked all angles
    Camber Angle (front)   RH 3°N   LH 2°N
    Camber Angle (rear)   RH 2½°N LH 2°N
    K.P.I.   RH 14½° LH 13½°

Driver's Comments:-

    Steering Lighter
    Car felt easier to handle

(This page and next) Technical report on a testing programme for the Triumph 2.5PI in December 1969 by Paddy Hopkirk and Brian Culcheth. This followed a promising 1-2-3 in the class on the RAC Rally, and with the London to Mexico World Cup Rally in mind scheduled for the following April.

- 2 -

Conclusion:-

The main problem at this stage seems to be the excessive body roll, and until this is controlled there is no way of improving the handling further, other than perhaps increasing the spring rates.

Action:-

Derek White of Standard Triumph has offered to investigate the possibility of fitting roll bars front and rear and is also obtaining higher rate springs for test purposes.

Attached:-

Times Taken

cc Derek White S.T.I. (Ride and Handling Executive)
    Peter Browning
    Les Needham
    Bill Price
    Doug Watts
    Cliff Humphries

Handling Tests on Triumph 2.5 P.I. MKII at Honiley 23/12/69

Weather	Dry and Cold	
Track	Damp	
Test 'A'	Hopkirk	40.2 secs.
		40.4
		40.2
		39.8
		40.0
		39.0
	Culcheth	44.2
		40.6
		39.4
		39.4
		40.8
		40.4
		41.6
Test 'B'	Hopkirk	38.8
		39.2
		39.2
		39.0
	Culcheth	39.2
		38.6
		39.6
		39.8
		40.6
		40.2
		42.4
		40.8
		39.0
Test 'C'	Hopkirk	38.6
		38.0
		38.6
		39.4
	Culcheth	39.2
		39.6
		39.2
		39.2
		39.2
		39.6
		40.2
		42.6
		40.2
Test 'D'	Hopkirk	38.2
		38.0
		39.2
	Culcheth	40.6
		39.4
		42.0
		39.8
Test 'E'	Hopkirk	39.4
	Culcheth	42.4
		39.4
		39.2
		38.2

1967 to 1970: THE END OF THE LINE by Peter Browning

Interview by Gerry Phillips — 1968

GP: There has been a lot of speculation about the future of the Competitions Department at Abingdon. How do you see your future?

PB: We have been rather amused by some of the fairy-tale plans that have appeared in print. When people start telling us how to run our affairs, perhaps it could be time to put the record straight.

Firstly, our plans for the future have not been formed without very careful thought. We have tried to research the value of motorsport. Those who eat, sleep and breath competitions can tend to get their ideas out of balance. It's no bad thing to have to sit back now and then and take a long, hard look at what we are trying to achieve.

Motorsport costs money, a lot of money, and nobody begrudges BL seeking a return for its investment. The benefits of motorsport can be so nebulous, you just cannot put them down on paper. You and I believe that our Monte successes have sold not just Minis in Europe, not only BMC cars in Europe, but have also brought tremendous British prestige. But you can't actually prove it. Your arguments can easily be knocked on the head when you consider that the best-selling car we have made – and it achieved 19 per cent of the total UK car sales – was the humble 1100, which has never done anything in motorsport. Yet one of our most successful cars in motorsport, which we have seen campaigned for almost ten years in international events, the big Healey, is taken out of production.

GP: So, what are your plans for rallying next year?

PB: Well, rallying is the most expensive activity in which we are involved, and over the past year it has sadly brought us the least return for our investment. Every manufacturer involved in international rallying has built an outright competition car to beat the Mini – only Porsche and Ford have really succeeded. Remember, our competition car is now some nine years old, and it was never really designed to thrash up and down the Alps, averaging speeds which the basic Mini, from which it is still very much derived, could never even achieve on a flat piece of road. Our rally successes over the past couple of years have only been possible because of super-human effort by everyone in the team. The drivers have really had to stick their necks out, the co-drivers have put in more and more effort in their recces and pace note making, the mechanics continue to work their customary miracles, and the development boys wring out a few more horses – from a poor little engine that began life in the A30.

We are forced to reduce our rallying activity, drastically. There is no point in soldiering on, supporting the sport just for the sake of it. It's better to drop out, surely, than be a second-rate team? However, we will be keeping our hand in, with rallying maybe a single car in selective events, where we have a good chance of success, or where the event can do us good in respect of local publicity.

Paddy Hopkirk is with us till the end of next year, so we will be using him for some rallying. Sadly, this is the end of the participation with the full works team, and I have had to indicate to Timo Makinen, Rauno Aaltonen and Tony Fall that we will not be in a position to retain them next year. I'm afraid the same goes for their co-drivers – Paul Easter, Henry Liddon and Mike Wood. It has been very sad for me to say goodbye to all this talent, probably the strongest team any manufacturer has ever had. I was particularly sorry when one of our national newspapers indicated that we had sacked the team. That was a most unfortunate word to use. We have never had signed contracts with any of our drivers, and both sides have been happy to operate under a gentleman's agreement. It was clear to all of our drivers and co-drivers that we were not going to be able to honour our side of the bargain which is to provide them with a winning car.

So, I have had no option but to release them to drive for other teams. Financially, we have rewarded our crews handsomely in the past, probably better than most. When you have the best drivers, they can demand the top rate.

continued overleaf

An interview by Gerry Phillips of Motoring News *done in October 1968 with a view to trying to clarify our plans at a time when there were mounting rumours about the future. Despite the fact that I thought I had toed the party line (and echoed much of the policy 'speak' coming to us from Longbridge), it was not published because it was not approved by the BL press office.*

But, a professional rally driver needs more than money to safeguard his future. He must be competing regularly in a competitive car, with more than a lucky chance of winning.

GP: What cars will you be using next year?

PB: We will continue with the Mini; it's still the most competitive car we have. I would like to widen this to investigate the rally potential of all the British Leyland models – the Rover 3500S, and the new fuel-injection two-litre Triumph are interesting possibilities. Our motorsport would need to form a worthwhile extension of British Leyland's marketing and development programmes – and as a test-bed to help sell parts through the Special Tuning Department.

GP: Will the London-Sydney Marathon be the last event this year for the team?

PB: Yes. Like most other British manufacturers, we are having to miss the RAC Rally simply because we just have not got time to prepare the cars, or cope with the organising demands. The Marathon is going to be our most demanding event ever. The clash of dates is most unfortunate, given that the RAC Rally is so important in terms of promoting the sport to the British public. I've also decided against doing the Monte next year, even though it's one event we could still win, if the weather is terrible. But it would be a gamble, and would require a large slice of our budget. And other rival team members might well be taking some key members of our team for the 1969 season, and would want them from the Monte onwards.

GP: What are your plans for the racing side of things?

PB: In the past, apart from the isolated MG entry, all our racing has been farmed out to teams like Cooper, British Vita and Donald Healey, but with a reduced rally programme, we have now got the facilities to do this ourselves at Abingdon. This makes good financial sense; there will be no factory sponsorship of other teams.

GP: So what will the racing be?

PB: I am personally a little anti-Championships, but would like to see a two-car Mini team compete in British and European Championship events. There are one or two non-Championship events which are of more use to us, more significant from the publicity or marketing points of view. There is little point in travelling half-way across Europe to chase two points of a Championship, if that country has no marketing of our products, for instance.

GP: What about the cars, are you looking at other Leyland models?

PB: Yes, I hope so. The MGC is a new model and has been showing promise and starting to get results. Unless you are going to enter racing with an out-and-out prestige sportscar, like the GT40, then I feel you are better to compete with the basic-shaped production car. The public's identification with the car seen on the track or in the photos is very important. It does not really matter to my mind what's under the bonnet, or if the car looks like an MGC or a Midget, so long as the public's automatic identification is with the model you are trying to sell. Ford, Mercedes and Jaguar have in the past proved that you can build a tremendous image with an out-and-out winner, but it's enormously costly. There can be no half measures: you cannot afford to settle for second best. As much as everyone would like to see Leyland involved in Grand Prix racing, the time and money would be better spent producing better models to sell from showrooms. BL is a company selling cars to the car-buying public, and our motorsport should reflect that marketing aim.

1967 to 1970: THE END OF THE LINE by Peter Browning

PRESS RELEASE

BRITISH LEYLAND MOTOR CORPORATION LIMITED
BERKELEY SQUARE HOUSE   BERKELEY SQUARE   LONDON W1

TELEPHONE:
01 - 499 6050
TELEX 22498

RELEASE IMMEDIATE: 25th August, 1970

BRITISH LEYLAND TO CLOSE COMPETITIONS DEPARTMENT

"British Leyland announces today that at the end of 1970 when the current
Years motor sport activities are at an end, the Competitions Department will be
closed."

For the last two years, it has been the declared policy of British Leyland
To only enter events from which maximum marketing and publicity benefit can be
Obtained. Although this has been generally achieved it has meant that a
Disproportionate amount of management time in the area of design development
And engineering has had to be devoted to competition at a time when the
Corporations forward model programme is being rapidly formed. It is now felt
That the new model programme must take precedence in the immediate future.
This decision does not preclude British Leylands possible entry into any sphere
Of motor sport in the future.

Re-entry would be considered in the context of British Leyland world
Wide requirements in marketing.

Commenting today George Turnbull, Deputy Managing Director of
British Leyland said:

"I should like to record our sincere gratitude and appreciation to
Peter Browning the Competitions Manager, who is leaving the Corporation
And to the Competitions Team at Abingdon, for all their hard work and
Dedication which has enabled us to record more successes than any other

/Continued . . . . .

The press release announcing the closure of the Competitions Department in August 1970. This was accompanied by a policy instruction to terminate the contracts of all of the drivers and co-drivers at the end of the year, and dispose of all of the then current fleet of works cars. Special Tuning was to continue and, as briefly covered in the Postscript chapter, competitions activities did continue from Abingdon until the MG factory was closed down in 1980.

Manufacturer over the past 16 years, and of course to all the famous crews.

We will continue to operate and expand the excellent facilities of
The Special Tuning Department at Abingdon. This department supplies an
Ever increasing range of factory approved conversion kits for both the private
Motorist and the sporting enthusiast who wish to improve the performance of
Their cars or participate in motor sport with British Leyland products.

(Confirmation of story issued to wire services last night - Monday 24 August)

BMC Competitions Department Secrets ...

Embarrassing first lap pit stop for the Andrew Hedges MGB in the 1966 Marathon at the Nürburgring after an off-circuit adventure into a field. Den Green is about to stem the flow from the holed fuel tank and repair the damaged lights. 84 hours later the team was celebrating an outright victory. This was one of the events where Peter Browning acted as pit manager before taking over from Stuart Turner.

1967 to 1970: THE END OF THE LINE by Peter Browning

Amongst Peter Browning's most rewarding events before taking over as Competitions Manager was running the three successful lone MGB entries at Le Mans in 1963, 1964 and 1965. In 1963 the MGB finished 12th overall and won its class despite spending an hour in the sand trap at Mulsanne. The following year the team finished 19th overall, won the Motor Trophy as the highest placed British car, and averaged 99.9mph (which generated more publicity than the magic 100mph!). In 1965 the MGB finished 11th overall and was runner-up in its class to a works Porsche which came into the pits on the last lap with a blown engine. This was MG's last entry in a major international race. Paddy Hopkirk drove all three years partnered by Alan Hutchinson in 1963 and Andrew Hedges in 1964 (photo) and 1965.

A young and somewhat apprehensive Peter Browning takes over the team in 1967 having initially told MG boss, John Thornley, that he really did not want the job. He was told not to argue and get on with it!

1967 to 1970: THE END OF THE LINE by Peter Browning

Overall runners-up and category winners on the 1967 Tulip Rally, Timo Makinen and Paul Easter.

Circuit of Ireland winner Paddy Hopkirk with Terry Harryman in 1967.

1967 to 1970: THE END OF THE LINE by Peter Browning

But for an uncharacteristic roll, Rauno Aaltonen and Henry Liddon, seen here picking up the pieces, might have finished higher than 3rd overall on the 1967 Swedish Rally.

Record-breaking at Monza in 1967 with the 1800. The car broke records at 92mph for 7 days and had to be slowed at the end because the BL press office did not want to publicise an unrealistic speed!

Peter Browning with Clive Baker, one of the 1967 Monza record-breaking team with the 1800.

1967 to 1970: THE END OF THE LINE by Peter Browning

The pair of 970 Mini-Coopers for the 1967 Marathon at the Nürburgring testing at Castle Combe. GRX5D – driven by Tony Fall, Julien Vernaeve and Andrew Hedges – finished 2nd overall.

Changing disc pads on the 970 Mini-Cooper in the 84 Hours Marathon at the Nürburgring in 1967. The Mini was the smallest engined car in the event, finishing 2nd overall and winning a special prize for spending the least time in the pits throughout the three-and-a-half day race.

BMC Competitions Department Secrets ...

Powerhouse of the last works big Healey prepared for the 1967 RAC Rally to be driven by Rauno Aaltonen. This was the ex-Morley 1964 Alpine car then owned by Peter Browning and the only big Healey available at the time. With its one-off lightweight, all-alloy engine and many special features Aaltonen rated this as the fastest and best handling big Healey of all time. Sadly, the car never ran as the Rally was cancelled at the last moment because of the foot and mouth crisis.

1967 to 1970: THE END OF THE LINE by Peter Browning

A visit to the Triumph factory at Coventry in 1968 as part of the evaluation of all the BL models and power units for possible competition use. Right to left: Peter Browning, Paddy Hopkirk, Competitions Foreman Doug Watts and, far left, Brian Culcheth.

BMC Competitions Department Secrets ...

The team's final Monte Carlo Rally was in 1968, when the Minis finished 3rd, 4th and 5th behind the dominating Porsches, and 1-2-3 in the category. This is Tony Fall and Mike Wood.

1967 to 1970: THE END OF THE LINE by Peter Browning

The controversial split Weber carburettors developed at Abingdon for the Mini-Cooper which nearly caused another Monte Carlo Rally fiasco in 1968.

The team of 1800s entered for the 1968 East African Safari in support of strong local dealer promotion for the car. Sadly, all three cars driven by Rauno Aaltonen, Timo Makinen and Tony Fall failed to finish.

Paddy Hopkirk, Tony Nash and Alec Poole in their 1800 leave the Crystal Palace start on the 1968 London to Sydney Marathon. They were to finish 2nd overall and all five works 1800s made it to Australia.

1967 to 1970: THE END OF THE LINE by Peter Browning

John Rhodes, unquestionably the fastest ever Mini racer, sideways as usual in the Abingdon race team car at the Silverstone Daily Express *Meeting in 1969.*

Fuel injection was the ultimate engine development on the rallying Mini-Coopers, and was used by Paddy Hopkirk to win his class on the 1969 Tour de France.

Start of the 1970 London to Mexico World Cup Rally in a packed Wembley Stadium for Australians Evan Green, Jack Murray and British journalist Hamish Cardno in the Triumph 2.5PI.

1967 to 1970: THE END OF THE LINE by Peter Browning

Brian Culcheth/Johnstone Syer deserved their 2nd overall with the Triumph 2.5PI on the 1970 London to Mexico World Cup Rally, having been responsible for all of the very demanding South American recce.

This Mini Clubman was entered in the 1970 London to Mexico World Cup Rally for John Handley and Paul Easter with BBC TV sponsorship. The objective was to go flat out and lead the rally in Europe to generate initial publicity, anticipating that most of the other crews would be saving themselves for the more serious sections in South America. Unfortunately, the Mini was an early retirement with piston failure.

1967 to 1970: THE END OF THE LINE by Peter Browning

Ladies' prize winners on the 1970 London to Mexico World Cup Rally were Rosemary Smith, Alice Watson and Ginette Derolland in this Austin Maxi. The ladies made the top 10 overall while the second Maxi, driven by members of the Red Arrows RAF Display Team, won its class.

The 1970 Scottish Rally was a rewarding event for the team with Brian Culcheth/Johnstone Syer winning outright in the Triumph 2.5 PI and Paddy Hopkirk/Tony Nash bringing this Mini Clubman 1275 GT into second place. The Clubman replaced the usual Mini-Cooper entry to try and promote the new model shape with a sporty image.

The special racing Rover 4.3 V8 which ran in the 1970 Marathon at the Nürburgring driven by Roy Pierpoint, Roger Enever and Clive Baker. The car was the sensation of the 86 Hours event but was withdrawn for safety reasons with prop shaft problems after 15 hours when over 50 miles ahead of all the works opposition. Just a week earlier BL had announced the closure of the Competitions Department.

1970-1980

Postscript

When the Competitions Department was closed down at the end of 1970, Special Tuning continued with Basil Wales in charge. Mainly through the enthusiasm of Brian Culcheth, the only member of the BMC/BL team to retain a promotional contract, a modest competitions programme was revived in 1971. Based around the use of the ex-World Cup Triumph 2.5 PI, Brian finished the Welsh and the Scottish, and was runner-up in Cyprus before winning his class with a Marina on the RAC Rally. A similar programme followed in 1972, the best result being a class win on the Safari with the Triumph, and in 1973 more sorties with the Marina.

BL's enthusiastic John Barber authorized significant changes in 1974 with Richard Seth-Smith replacing Basil Wales, and heading up an expanded new team at Abingdon which included the return of experienced Bill Price (former assistant to Marcus Chambers, Stuart Turner and Peter Browning) to the position of Workshop Supervisor. The Dolomite Sprint now headed the rally programme supported by selected Marina entries (with Unipart sponsorship), while Broadspeed received support to campaign the Dolomite in the British Saloon Car Championship.

Culcheth led the rallying Dolomite team through 1975 to 1977 picking up class wins in mainly national events with Bill Price now promoted to Team Manager. The TR7 rally programme commenced at this time in the hands of Tony Pond.

1977 saw the arrival of John Davenport as the new boss at Abingdon, The TR7 V8 was powered from 1978, and campaigned with tremendous skill by Tony Pond, with invited drives in 1980 by Timo Makinen and Roger Clark.

Closure of the MG Car Company by BL in 1980 brought the end of the last decade of competitions at Abingdon. John Davenport persuaded BL to set up a new department at Cowley to run the ambitious MG Metro 6R4 rally programme, but this, too, came to an end in 1987 with the demise of Group B rallying.

The Special Tuning prepared Marina 1.3 driven by Brian Culcheth and Johnstone Syer on the 1000 Lakes Rally in 1973 just missed a class win by 14 seconds, but won it in 1974.

Setting fastest time on the Eppynt stage on the 1975 Tour of Britain, Brian Culcheth and Ray Hutton in the Triumph Dolomite Sprint finished 2nd overall.

1970 to 1980: Postscript

Tony Pond scored many spectacular successes with the Triumph TR7 V8 for the renamed Leyland ST team from 1978 until closure of the Abingdon factory in 1980.

Roll of Honour

OUTRIGHT WINS 1955-1980

1956/7
Ladies Champion: Nancy Mitchell

1958
Ladies Champion: Pat Moss

1960
Liège: Pat Moss (AH 3000)

1961
Alpine: Don Morley (AH 3000)

1962
Tulip: Pat Moss (Mini-Cooper)
Alpine: Don Morley (AH 3000)
Baden Baden: Pat Moss (Mini-Cooper)

1963
Alpine: Rauno Aaltonen (Mini-Cooper)

1964
Monte: Paddy Hopkirk (Mini-Cooper)
Tulip: Timo Makinen (Mini-Cooper)
Austrian: Paddy Hopkirk (AH 3000)
Liège: Rauno Aaltonen (AH 3000)

1965
Monte: Timo Makinen (Mini-Cooper)
Circuit: Paddy Hopkirk (Mini-Cooper)
Guards 1000: John Rhodes/Warwick Banks (MGB)
Geneva: Rauno Aaltonen (Mini-Cooper)
Czech: Rauno Aaltonen (Mini-Cooper)
Polish: Rauno Aaltonen (Mini-Cooper)
1000 Lakes: Timo Makinen (Mini-Cooper)
Three Cities: Rauno Aaltonen (Mini-Cooper)
RAC: Rauno Aaltonen (Mini-Cooper)

European Champion: Rauno Aaltonen
1966
Circuit: Tony Fall (Mini-Cooper)
Tulip: Rauno Aaltonen (Mini-Cooper)
Austrian: Paddy Hopkirk (Mini-Cooper)
Scottish: Tony Fall (Mini-Cooper)
Czech: Rauno Aaltonen (Mini-Cooper)
Polish: Tony Fall (Mini-Cooper)
Marathon: Julien Vernaeve/Andrew Hedges (MGB)
1000 Lakes: Timo Makinen (Mini-Cooper)
Three Cities: Timo Makinen (Mini-Cooper)

1967
Monte: Rauno Aaltonen (Mini-Cooper)
Circuit: Paddy Hopkirk (Mini-Cooper)
Acropolis: Paddy Hopkirk (Mini-Cooper)
Geneva: Tony Fall (Mini-Cooper)
Danube: Tony Fall (Austin 1800)
1000 Lakes: Timo Makinen (Mini-Cooper)
Alpine: Paddy Hopkirk (Mini-Cooper)

1969
Saltzburgring: John Rhodes (Mini-Cooper)

1970
Scottish: Brian Culcheth (Triumph 2.5)

1977
Boucles de Spa: Tony Pond (Triumph TR7)

1978
Ypres: Tony Pond (Triumph TR7 V8)
Manx: Tony Pond (Triumph TR7 V8)

1980
Ypres: Tony Pond (Triumph TR7 V8)
Manx: Tony Pond (Triumph TR7 V8)

ROLL OF HONOUR

CLASS WINNING DRIVERS
Rauno Aaltonen, Derek Astle, Clive Baker, Warwick Banks, Emmett Brown, Mike Christie, Andrew Cowan, Brian Culcheth, Per Eklund, Roger Enever, Peter Evans, Tony Fall, Jack Flaherty, Tommy Gold, John Handley, Andrew Hedges, Paddy Hopkirk, Alan Hutchinson, Dick Jacobs, Douglas Johns, Joan Johns, Rupert Jones, Harry Kallstrom, Terry Kingsley, Jorma Lusenius, Roger Mac, Timo Makinen, Peter Manton, Pauline Mayman, Nancy Mitchell, Don Morley, David Seigle-Morris, Rosemary Smith, Logan Morrison, Pat Moss, Jim Parkinson, Alec Poole, Tony Pond, John Rhodes, Peter Riley, Pat Ryan, Jack Sears, Julien Vernaeve, Lars Ytterbring, Sobieslaw Zasada.

CLASS WINNING CO-DRIVERS
Tony Ambrose, Don Barrow, Christabel Carlisle, Willy Cave, Brian Coyle, Ron Crellin, Brian Culcheth, Val Domleo, Lofty Drews, Paul Easter, Ross Finlay, Fred Gallagher, Peter Garnier, John Gittings, Terry Harryman, Mike Hughes, Joan Johns, Rupert Jones, Pekko Keskitalo, Attis Krauklis, Henry Liddon, Pauline Mayman, Philip Morgan, Erle Morley, Tony Nash, Mike Nicholson, Gunnar Palm, Lars Persson, Dave Richards, Peter Roberts, Mike Scarlett, Jack Scott, John Steadman, Johnstone Syer, Stuart Turner, Ann Wisdom, Mike Wood.

OTHER BOOKS BY THE SAME AUTHORS

Marcus Chambers
Works Wonders: BMC and Rootes – ISBN 0-947981-94-2

Stuart Turner
Twice Lucky – ISBN 1 85960-602-4
Harnessing Horsepower – ISBN 978-1-845843-06-9

Peter Browning
Healeys and Austin-Healeys – ISBN 0 85429 209 8
The Jenson Healey Stories – ISBN 0 900549 21 1
Works Minis – ISBN 0 85429 967 X
Works Big Healeys – ISBN 0 85429 966 1
Works MGs (with Mike Allison) – ISBN 0 85960 603 2

Also from Veloce:

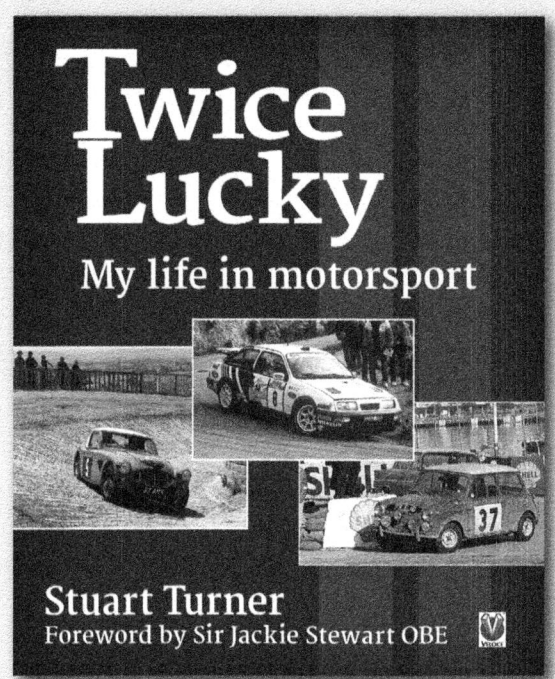

The fascinating, funny, sometimes controversial autobiography of Stuart Turner, one of the leading motorsport figures of the past 50 years. In this book, one of motorsport's most engaging and enthusiastic characters writes frankly, revealingly and above all modestly about guiding BMC and Ford to rally glory.

Now available as an eBook

Available to download from:

http://digital.veloce.co.uk/ebooks/eV4531.html

Flowing layout • 70 pictures
From £9.99
ISBN: 978-1-845845-31-5
UPC: 6-36847-04531-9

See **www.digital.veloce.co.uk** for our complete range of eBooks

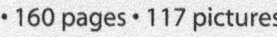

This book covers the life of one of the greatest women rally drivers of all time, Pat Moss Carlsson.

Sister to Stirling Moss, Pat had a highly successful career in show-jumping before moving into motorsport, going on to become European Ladies Rally Champion no fewer than five times.

ISBN: 978-1-845843-06-9
Hardback • 25x20.7cm
• £24.99* UK/$49.95* USA
• 160 pages • 117 pictures

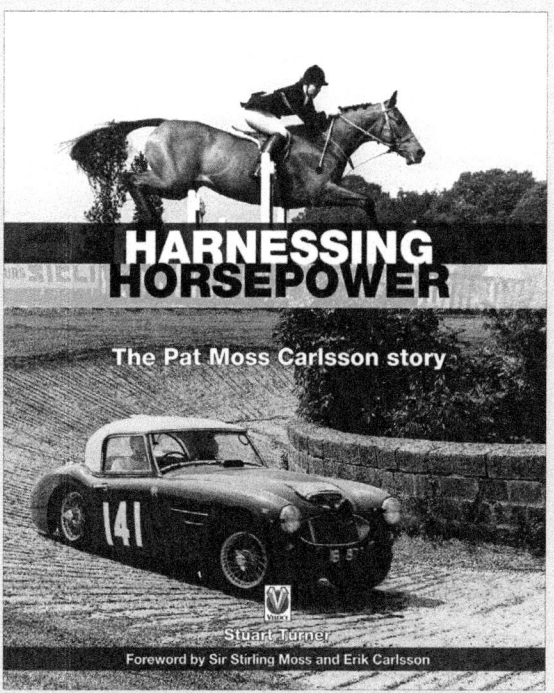

For more info on Veloce titles, visit our website at www.veloce.co.uk
• email: info@veloce.co.uk
• Tel: +44(0)1305 260068
* prices subject to change, p&p extra

The Escort RS Cosworth, which began rallying in 1993, was one of the most ingenious designs of all time, and eventually became Ford's most successful model since the legendary Escorts of the 1970s. The combination of Cosworth power, four-wheel-drive transmission, and an effective aerodynamic package made it a Rally Giant in all conditions, and, until the all-new Focus WRC was launched in 1999, this generation of Escorts was the most effective rally car that Ford had ever produced.

ISBN: 978-1-84584-181-2
Paperback • 19.5x21cm • £14.99* UK/$29.95* USA
• 128 pages • 146 colour and b&w pictures

The HF 4WD – a compact, five-door Lancia – dominated world-class rallying for six years, winning innumerable events, World Championships for Drivers, and World Championships for Manufacturers. Alongside the cars, driving heroes such as Markku Alan, Didier Auriol, Miki Biasion, Juha Kankkunen and Carlos Sainz also became legendary in this period.
The Integrale was both the most successful rally car ever produced by Lancia, and the last, for when the car came to the end of its career in 1993, the company finally and irrevocably withdrew from the sport.

ISBN: 978-1-845842-58-1
Paperback • 19.5x21cm • £15.99* UK/$29.95* USA
• 128 pages • 108 colour and b&w pictures

This book describes the birth, development, and rallying career of the BMC Mini-Cooper/Mini-Cooper in the 1960s, providing a compact and authoritative history of where, when and how it became so important to the sport.

ISBN: 978-1-845841-83-6
Paperback • 19.5x21cm
• £15.99* UK/$29.95* USA
• 128 pages • 126 colour and b&w pictures

For more information visit www.veloce.co.uk

How the giant-killing Minis of rallying, rallycross & racing fame were converted from standard Mini-Coopers in the BMC Competitions Department. The author, who spent 22 years in 'Comps', reveals the secrets of specification, build technique and development of the world famous Works Minis.

ISBN: 978-1-845848-70-5
Paperback • 25x20.7cm • £19.99* UK/$35* USA • 96 pages • pictures

Lasting six weeks, and covering 16,000 miles from London to Mexico City via some of the most varying, tortuous and difficult terrain on three continents, the 1970 World Cup Rally was a unique high-speed event, attracting many serious works teams such as Ford and British Leyland. Despite the tremendous amounts of money spent choosing and developing new cars, completing months-long route surveys, and analysing every detail of diets, oxygen provision, and the number of crew members, out of an entry of more than 100 cars, only 23 cars made it to the finish.
It was then, and remains now, the toughest rally of all time.

ISBN: 978-1-845842-71-0
Hardback • 25x25cm • £35* UK/$69.95* USA • 208 pages • 237 colour and b&w pictures

prices subject to change, p&p extra

• email: info@veloce.co.uk • Tel: +44(0)1305 260068

Index

Alpine-Renault 141, 144
Andersson, Ove 144
Austin (and models) 71, 88, 145 :
　1800 71, 88, 93, 124
　A30 11
　A35 8, 10, 11, 23, 40
　A40 10, 11, 45, 50, 52, 53, 105
　A50 20, 36
　A90 Westminster 7, 8, 20, 31, 33, 34
　A105 Westminster 41
　A110 Westminster 62, 83, 85
　Allegro 145
　Maxi 179
Austin Healey Club 138, 140
Austin-Healey models:
　100S 9
　100-Six 12, 41
　3000 12, 51, 55, 58, 60, 61, 64, 67, 71, 84, 86, 106, 109, 114, 115, 116, 121, 123, 125, 128, 131,139, 140, 147, 170
　Sprite 10, 12, 45, 59, 61, 71, 91, 105
Autosport 138

Bagshot Military Testing Ground 145
Barber, John 181
Barnes, Col Stanley 41
Baxter, Raymond 63, 140, 141
Beatles, The 61
Bentley 6
BMC Competitions Committee 6, 14, 79, 88, 89, 98
BMC Competitions Reunion Dinner 149
BMC 'works' drivers and co-drivers :
　Aaltonen, Rauno 60, 62, 67, 113, 122, 126, 129, 133, 135, 136, 140, 141, 167, 170 173
　Ambrose, Tony 52, 53, 86, 122, 129, 133
　Appleyard, Ian 8, 12
　Appleyard, Paul 8
　Asbury, Stan 31
　Astle, Derek 12, 58, 60
　Baker, Clive 168, 180
　Barrow, Don 121
　Baxter, Raymond 63, 95
　Bensted-Smith, Dick 35
　Brookes, Ray 42, 44
　Brooks, John 31, 42
　Burgess, Gerry 33, 35
　Cardno, Hamish 176
　Carlisle, Christabel 61, 114
　Cave, Willy 7, 12, 21, 31
　Clark, Roger 181
　Collinson, Alan 31
　Couper, Mike 34
　Cowan, Andrew 146
　Croft-Pearson, Sam 33, 35
　Culcheth, Brian 113, 138, 146, 147, 157, 171, 177, 179, 181, 182
　Derolland, Ginette 179
　Domleo, Val 122
　Easter, Paul 127, 132, 165, 178
　Edwards, Courtenay 124
　Elford, Vic 12
　Enever, Roger 139, 180
　Fall, Tony 101, 120, 136, 141, 169, 172, 173
　Faichney, Pat 27
　Finnemore, Freddie 31
　Gott, John 8, 10, 12, 26, 28, 29, 35, 43, 44, 46, 67, 78, 85
　Green, Evan 176
　Hall, Anne 35, 41
　Handley, John 147, 178
　Harryman, Terry 166
　Hedges, Andrew 109, 139, 162, 163, 169
　Holt, Geoff 31, 32, 39
　Holt, Reg 31
　Hopkirk, Paddy 60, 62, 64, 68, 109, 113, 116, 118, 119, 134, 140, 143, 146, 157, 163, 166, 171, 174, 176, 179
　Hutchinson, Alan 163
　Hutton, Ray 182
　Jacobs, Dick 9, 19
　James, Ken 12
　Johns, Joan 7, 33, 39
　Johns, Douglas 45
　Jones, Rev Rupert 12, 108
　Kallstrom, Harry 135
　Liddon, Henry 118, 119, 134, 136 141, 167
　Mabbs, Geoff 61, 146, 147
　Macklin, Lance 9
　Makinen, Timo 60, 62, 77, 112, 114, 115, 117, 121, 127, 129, 132, 137, 140, 141, 154, 165, 173, 181
　Mayman, Pauline 122
　Milne, Johnny 12, 35, 46
　Mitchell, Nancy 9, 35, 37, 39, 41
　Moore, Sam 31
　Morley, Donald 12, 25, 49, 57, 60, 62, 70, 78, 108, 118, 123, 125, 126, 137, 170
　Morley, Erle 12, 49, 57, 60, 70, 78, 118, 123, 125, 126, 137, 170
　Morris-Goodall, Mortimer 31
　Morrison, Logan 113
　Moss, Pat 8, 11, 12, 27, 33, 37, 41, 45, 47, 48, 50, 52, 55, 56, 59, 60, 70, 110, 138
　Moss, Stirling 6, 8, 21
　Murray, Jack 176
　Nash, Tony 174, 179
　Neal, Steve 147
　Olthoff, Bob 109
　Ozanne, Pat 12
　Pierpoint, Roy 148, 180
　Pitt, Alec 12
　Pond, Tony 181, 183
　Poole, Alec 139, 174
　Rhodes, John 147, 175
　Rich, Doreen 33
　Riley, Peter 53, 105
　Roberts, Peter 58
　Sears, Jack 12, 36, 109
　Seigle-Morris, David 12, 13, 52, 58, 60
　Shaw, Len 31
　Smith, Rosemary 179
　Spice, Gordon 147
　Sprinzel, John 12, 52, 59, 78, 124, 138
　Sutcliffe, Mike 12
　Syer, Johnstone 146, 177, 179, 182
　Tooley, Chris 35

Turner, Stuart 12
Vernaeve, Julien 139, 169
Wadsworth, John 85
Walker, Ian 33
Watson, Alice 179
Wharton, Ken 9, 36
Williamson, John 12
Wisdom, Ann 12, 27, 41, 45, 50, 51, 52, 110
Wisdom, Elsie ('Bill') 7, 15
Wisdom, Tommy 7, 45, 124
Whitmore, Sir John 109
Wood, Mike 85, 101, 136, 172
Boddy, Bill 59
Bohringer, Eugen 60, 61
BRDC 138
Britannia aircraft 146
British Caledonian Airways 146
British Saloon Car Championship 147, 181
BRM 6
Broadspeed 181
Brown, John 52
Brown, Mrs 41
Browning, Peter 62, 91, 125, 162, 164, 168, 170, 171, 181
BTRDA 78

Cambridge University Automobile Club 10
Carlsson, Erik 12, 55, 56, 59, 61, 67, 111, 128
Castle Combe race circuit 148, 169
Castrol oil company 7, 40, 62, 63, 81, 141
Challis, Neville 144
Chalmers. Stan 131, 140
Chambers, Marcus 10, 37, 39, 60, 138, 148, 181
Chambers, Mrs Pat 9
Chapman, Rod 94
Clark, Roger 63
Clayton, Ann 64
Collins, Peter 6
Colonial Development Corporation 6
Cooper, John 60, 63, 67, 75, 91, 147
Cooper Car Company 147
Cousins, Cecil 7
CUAC drivers:
  Aley, John 11
  Horrocks, Gyde 11
  Jones, Rev Rupert 11
  Riviere, Peter 11
  Simpson, Ray 11, 40
  Taylor, Arthur 11
  Threlfall, Tom 11

Daimler (and models) 9
Daniels, Jack 61
Davenport, John 144, 181
Davis, S C H ('Sammy') 6, 9
Dixon, David 52
Donald Healey Motor Company 147
Dorland Advertising 63, 140
Dunlop tyres 10, 11, 29, 54, 62, 103, 126, 137, 139, 141

Enever, Syd 7, 31, 145
Equipe Nationale Belge 139
European Rally Championship 129
European Touring Car Ladies' Award 39

Falin, Raoul 61
Fangio, Juan-Manuel 61
Ferrari 62, 139
FIA 141, 143
Financial Times 147
Ford (and models) 11, 60, 63, 71, 89, 94, 115, 139, 144, 146, 147
Frazer Nash 8

Gardner, Doug 137
Gardner, Jack 137

Hamblin, Doug 10
Harriman, Sir George 14, 68, 69
Harrow Car Club 138
Hawthorn, Mike 6
Hayes, Walter 63
Hayter, Don 145
Healey, Donald 60, 71
Healey, Geoffrey 91, 139, 147
Hiam, David 29, 62
Higgins, Norman 60, 137
Hill, Graham 61
Hill, Jimmy 131
Hillman (and models) 147
Hounslow, Alec 7, 59
HRG 6, 8, 9, 37
Humphries, Cliff 10, 141

Ickx, Jacky 139
Issigonis, Alec 61, 67, 69, 93

Jackson, Reg 7
Jaguar (and models) 8, 145
Jenkinson, Denis 21, 59

Kemsley, Jack 142
Kendrick, George 41
Kimber, Cecil 137
Knowldale Car Club 61, 77

Lambourne, Les 137
Lancia (and models) 144
Levegh, Pierre 9
Leyland ST 183
Ljungfeldt, Bo 61
Lord, Sir Leonard 9

McComb, Wilson 76, 92, 138
McQueen, Steve 68
Maher, Eddie 75
Mann, Alan 139
Martin, Charlie 137
Mechanics at Abingdon:
  Bartram, Pete 85
  Bradford, Stan 130
  Brown, Roy 130
  Evans, Johnny 130
  Green, Den 10, 130, 139, 162
  Hall, Nobby 130
  Hogan, Mick 130
  Moylan, Brian 130
  Organ, Johnny 130
  Owen, Brian 130
  Partridge, Mike 130
  Pike, Dudley 130
  Vokins, Robin 62, 130
  Watts, Doug 9, 11, 60, 130, 137, 143, 146, 171
  Wellman, Tommy 10, 130
  Bob Whittington 130
  Gerald Wiffen 130
Mercedes-Benz (and models) 9, 61
MG Car Club 7, 8, 39, 138
MG models:
  K3 Magnette 7
  M-Type Midget 7
  MGA 6, 20, 35, 37, 105, 108, 109
  MGA Le Mans car (EX182) 7, 9, 19, 20, 22
  MGA Twin-Cam 43, 44, 46
  MGB 62, 118, 122, 139, 140, 162, 163
  MGC 71
  Metro 6R4 181
  Midget 11, 58, 105
  TF 8, 16, 27
  YB 8
  ZA Magnette 7, 9, 20, 21, 31, 32, 38
Mikkola, Hannu 79, 146
Mini models:
  850 11, 12, 48, 49, 59, 108
  Mini-Cooper 60, 61, 62, 105, 106, 110, 113
  Mini-Cooper S 49, 62, 63, 70, 79, 85, 88, 91, 101, 104, 111, 116, 118, 120, 125, 126, 131, 136, 140, 141,

143, 148, 169, 172, 173, 175, 176
  Clubman 1275GT 178, 179
Mini-Cooper Register 138
Mitchell, Terry 145
Montlhery race circuit 11, 40
Mont Ventoux 62
Moore, Don 63, 75, 91
Morris (and models) 12, 47, 48, 61, 62, 67, 71, 138, 141, 145
  1800 145, 146, 151, 154, 167, 168, 173, 174
  Marina 145, 181, 182
Morris-Goodall, Mortimer 9
Motor trophy 164
Motoring News 13, 59, 159
Motor Sport 59
Moulton bicycles 139

Nash, Ralph 146
Nuffield Competitions Committee 6
Nuvolari, Tazio 7, 59

Overseas Food Corporation 6

Phillips, Gerry 159
Porsche (and models) 62, 9, 141, 143,144, 148, 163, 172
Prescott hillclimb 36
Price, Bill 10, 62, 130, 181

Races:
  Eight Clubs, Silverstone 38, 138
  86 Hour Marathon (Nurburgring) 148, 162, 169, 180
  Le Mans 6, 8, 9, 17, 19, 140, 147, 163
  Mille Miglia 21
  Monza 167, 168
  Nurburgring 139, 148, 162, 169, 180
  Sebring 30, 62, 91, 139
  Targa Florio 139
  Tour de France 67, 68, 176
  Tourist Trophy (Ulster) 9, 22
Rallies:
  1000 Lakes 182
  (French) Alpine 9, 11, 12, 28, 29, 41, 46, 59, 64, 67, 99, 136, 170
  Canadian 67
  Cats Eyes 48
  Circuit of Ireland 8, 166

Cyprus 181
East African Safari 80, 173
Flowers (SanRemo) 143
German 12, 25
Liege-Rome-Liege 12, 35, 41, 43, 44, 51, 59, 60, 70
Liege-Sofia-Liege 82, 86, 90, 99, 121, 122
London 7
London-Mexico World Cup Rally 145, 147, 156, 157, 176, 178, 179, 181
London – Sydney Marathon 63, 145, 146, 151, 152, 154, 174
Lyon-Charbonnieres 37
Mini Miglia 12, 48
Mobil Economy Run 41
Monte Carlo 7, 8, 10, 16, 21, 31, 33, 34, 42, 45, 46, 49, 50, 52, 54, 59, 61, 62, 90, 93, 95, 97, 101, 103, 105, 108, 113, 119, 124, 134, 137, 139, 143, 172, 173
Police 98
Polish 60
RAC (British) 8, 11, 12, 16, 27, 36, 47, 52, 55, 61, 62, 67, 112, 122, 123, 125, 129, 135, 146, 156, 157, 170, 181
Rally des Cimes 94
Scottish 146, 156, 179, 181
Swedish 167
Tour de Corse 148
Tour of Britain 182
Tulip 7, 32, 38, 110, 125, 165
Viking 11, 12
Welsh 181
Range Rover 146, 147
Red Arrows Display Team 179
Richardson, Ken 6, 8, 9
Riley (and models) 36, 42
Rootes Group 6
Rover (and models) 145, 146, 148, 180
Royal Air Force 78

Saab (and models) 12, 59, 67, 69, 111
Safety Fast 138
Seth-Smith, Richard 181
Shaw, Bill 148
Silverstone 63, 91, 138, 175

Simpson, Ray 131
Smith, John 131, 140
Special Tuning Department 95, 144, 155, 161, 182
Speight, Oliver 54
Sprinzel, John 10
Standard (and models) 8, 11, 60
Stewart, Jackie 63, 91
Stokes, Lord 146
Suez Crisis 11
Suffield, Lester 62, 73, 95, 98
Sunbeam (and models) 10
Sunday Night at the London Palladium 61, 62, 119

That Was The Week That Was 76
Thornley, John 6, 7, 9, 12, 13, 18, 19, 21, 22, 39, 59, 60, 62, 64, 67, 69, 72, 74, 98, 131, 137, 139, 147, 148, 164
'Three Musketeers' 8, 31
Triumph (and models) 6, 8, 11, 27, 144, 145, 171
  2.5PI 145, 146, 156, 157, 176, 177, 179, 181
  Dolomite Sprint 181, 182
  TR7 V8 181, 183
Turnbull, George 148
Turner, Margaret 62
Turner, Stuart 12, 13, 46, 48, 106, 112, 131, 137, 140, 148, 162, 181
Twice Lucky 63
Tyresoles retreads 34
Tyrrell, Ken 63, 67, 91

Vanden Plas Princess 4-Litre R 89, 125, 143
Veteran Car Club 138
Vintage Sports Car Club 138

Wales, Basil 145, 181
Walker, Murray 147
Wolseley (and models) 10
Wright, Pamela 41